Getty-Dubay Italic Calligraphy for School & Home

∞

Inga Dubay

This book belongs to

_____

Getty-Dubay Productions · Portland, Oregon · USA

I dedicate this book to the honor and memory of Lloyd J. Reynolds, who inspired me and many others to fall in love with letters. My thanks to the teachers and students whose love of letters encouraged me to write this book and also to Barbara Getty, my dear friend and collaborator of over 40 years.

GETTY-DUBAY ITALIC HANDWRITING SERIES (8 Books: A-G for Kindergarten to Grade 6 and beyond, Instruction Manual), Barbara Getty and Inga Dubay. Portland State University, Continuing Education Press, Portland, Oregon. 1980; Second Edition, 1986; Third Edition, 1994; Getty-Dubay Productions, Portland, Oregon. Fourth Edition, 2009-2016.

ITALIC LETTERS: CALLIGRAPHY & HANDWRITING, Inga Dubay and Barbara Getty. Van Nostrand Reinhold Company, Inc., New York, New York. 1984; Portland State University, Continuing Education Press, Portland, Oregon, Revised Edition, 1992.

WRITE NOW: GETTY-DUBAY ITALIC HANDWRITING (55-minute DVD) Getty-Dubay Productions, Portland, Oregon, 1996, 2005. 2009-2015

WRITE NOW: THE GETTY-DUBAY PROGRAM FOR HANDWRITING SUCCESS, Barbara Getty and Inga Dubay. Portland State University, Continuing Education Press, Portland, Oregon. 1991. Revised Edition, 2005; Getty-Dubay Productions, Portland, Oregon, Third Edition, 2016.

GETTY-DUBAY ITALIC CALLIGRAPHY: for School & Home
Inga Dubay
©2016 Getty-Dubay. All rights reserved.

This text may not be reproduced in whole or in part without the express written permission of the copyright holder.

ISBN: 978-0-9827762-6-1

The following acknowledgements are gratefully recognized:
Anita Bigelow, Alice Chan, Deborah Davis, Jonathan Dubay, Joseph Dubay, Walter Englert, Ruth Frankel, Barbara Getty, Nancy Halliburton, Susan Hauser, Mackenzie Jeans, Ted Kaye, Gregory MacNaughton, Marianne Nelson, Robert Palladino, Joanna Priestley, Stephanie Snyder, Letitia Wulff.

Reed College Critical Practice Institute, Portland Public School Elementary School teachers: Brian Aase, Lisa Barnett, Kori Bass, Sarah Clark, Deziré Clarke, Gregory Clarkson, Paul Colvin, Renee Espinoza, Jonathon Fischer, Suzanne Germaneri-Clarkson, Nancy Gilkey, Elizabeth Israel-Davis, Meredith Jue, Rachel Kyriss, Madeleine Mininger, Carolyn Neal, Linda Nichenko, Dawn Roberts, Natalie Speer, Heather Torain, Lisa Van Clock, Zachary Vestal, Jamie Williams, Sharese Williams. Holly Denman, Principal, Cascade Heights Public Charter School.

Font design (text): Lucida Schoolbook Family by Kris Holmes and Charles Bigelow (Monotype).
Font design (italic letterforms & numerals): Jonathan Dubay and Inga Dubay.

Library of Congress Control Number: 2015916920

Published by Getty-Dubay Productions, LLC
Portland, Oregon USA
www.handwritingsuccess.com

Distributed by Allport Editions
716 NE Lawrence Avenue, Portland, Oregon 97232 USA
800-777-2844 info@allport.com

Printed by Brown Printing Inc., Portland, Oregon, with vegetable-based no-VOC inks on papers containing sustainable harvest wood fibers and a minimum 30% post-consumer waste.

Printed in the United States of America

Cover photo: Mt. Hood and Trillium Lake, Oregon USA

TABLE OF CONTENTS

Preface   4
Introduction   5
The Edged Pen & Other Materials   6
Mechanics, Experimenting with the Edged Pen   7
Classroom Management   8
Supplementary Materials, Golden Ratio   9
Historical Charts   10
Cards & Letters   11
Variations & Improvisations, Pen Play   12
Glossary   13

3.5 mm nib   14-50

	Historical Chart	Worksheet
Lowercase Family 1 (i l j) and Family 2 (x only)	14	15
Lowercase Family 2 (k v w x z)	16	17
Lowercase Family 3 (n h m r)	18	19
Lowercase Family 4 (u y)	20	21
Lowercase Family 5 (a d g q)	22	23
Lowercase Family 6 (b p)	24	25
Lowercase Family 7 (o e c s)	26	27
Lowercase Family 8 (f t)	28	29

Review Lowercase, Pangram, Punctuation   30-31

	Historical Chart	Worksheet
Formal Capitals A B C	32	33
Formal Capitals D E F	34	35
Formal Capitals G H I	36	37
Formal Capitals J K L	38	39
Formal Capitals M N O	40	41
Formal Capitals P Q R	42	43
Formal Capitals S T U	44	45
Formal Capitals V W X	46	47
Formal Capitals Y Z	48	49

Hindu-Arabic Numerals   50

2mm nib   51-59

Review, Ligatures   51
Plain Capitals, Small Capitals & Mixed Capitals   52
Poem   53
Quotations   54
Quotations   55
Greek & Latin Root Words   56
Fifty Most Used English Words   57
Cards & Letters, Flourished Capitals & Lowercase   58
Cursive Italic   59

Ruled Lines   60-64

Lowercase Historical Chart 3.5mm nib   60
Lowercase 3.5mm nib (14mm body height)   61
Capitals Historical Chart 3.5mm nib   62
Capitals 3.5mm nib (14mm body height)   63
Capitals & Lowercase 2mm nib (8mm body height)   64

PREFACE

The book you are holding was developed in collaboration with a group of talented and dedicated Portland Public School teachers from more than ten different schools. These teachers gathered at Reed College each month for three years to study italic handwriting and calligraphy under the direction of Inga Dubay. This special workshop was organized as part of the Critical Practice Institute, a branch of the Calligraphy Initiative in honor of Lloyd J. Reynolds at the Douglas F. Cooley Memorial Art Gallery, Reed College's visual art museum and the home of Reed's newly reborn calligraphy activities.

The Calligraphy Initiative is named after visionary professor Lloyd J. Reynolds (1902-1978), who introduced the practice of Italic handwriting and calligraphy at Reed College and throughout the Pacific Northwest. Reynolds taught at Reed for forty years, as well as the Portland Art Museum, Marylhurst College, and a host of other places. Reynolds also taught calligraphy in public schools throughout Portland. He devoted himself to imparting the art of beautiful writing to school teachers so that they too could instill it in their students. Reynolds' mission, to share his love of calligraphy and paleography, continues through this wonderful book. Reynolds was Inga Dubay's calligraphy teacher, and Inga is a vital part of his legacy.

There is much of Lloyd Reynolds in this book. Reynolds spoke often of his beloved "three Bills": William Blake, William Morris, and William Shakespeare. Like Reynolds, Blake was a poet, engraver, book artist, and deeply spiritual man. William Morris was the founder of the British Arts and Crafts movement. Morris designed wallpaper and furniture, and was a renowned book artist and calligrapher. Morris's insistence on the importance of crafting things by hand was a great inspiration to Reynolds. Finally, William Shakespeare needs no introduction; anyone who loves literature and the sound of poetic language knows the work of Shakespeare.

Following the example of Reynolds, Inga has included quotations by Blake and Shakespeare in the book. The spirit of William Morris is here too. One of the first things Inga ever shared with us is this quote by Morris: "The true secret of happiness lies in taking a genuine interest in all the details of daily life, (and) in elevating them by art." Morris wanted, above all else, for people to be employed in work that was both useful and fulfilling, the kind of work that ennobles the worker and instills sincere pride in a job well done.

That's what Inga wants, too, for teachers and students to discover the joy and wisdom of calligraphy, and the history of the alphabet, and to employ their minds as well as their hands in the making of beautiful and useful things.

Gregory MacNaughton
Education Outreach and Calligraphy Initiative Coordinator
Douglas F. Cooley Memorial Art Gallery
Reed College
Portland, Oregon

Stephanie Snyder
John and Anne Hauberg Curator and Director
Douglas F. Cooley Memorial Art Gallery
Reed College
Portland, Oregon

INTRODUCTION

So many good things come from the study of italic calligraphy. Moving a pen across the paper to create letters develops hand/eye coordination and fine motor skills while improving left-brain/right-brain synergy. Even second graders, the youngest students for whom this teaching program is designed, reap myriad benefits from calligraphy's engaging pace and the personal rewards from creating beautiful letterforms with their own hands.

This program introduces second grade students on up to italic calligraphy and its history. Italic letters have been used for centuries in human communication. Students will discover the enjoyment of forming letters that through history have been both functional and beautiful, made robust here by using a body height of four pen widths (see Variations & Improvisations) and shortened ascenders and descenders which match those found in everyday italic handwriting. The calligraphy you see in Getty-Dubay Italic Calligraphy is my own, captured digitally as a font for the creation of this book.

This italic calligraphy program, which utilizes the edged pen, builds upon the lessons of the Getty-Dubay Italic Handwriting Series, originally published in 1980 by Portland State University Continuing Education Press. The prototype for Getty-Dubay Italic Calligraphy was first used in 2009 at the ACCESS Academy in Portland, Oregon, for second and third graders whose introduction to italic letter shapes had been by using the workbooks of the Getty-Dubay Italic Handwriting Series.

My suggestion is for you to do the same, to use Getty-Dubay Italic Calligraphy along with the Getty-Dubay Italic Handwriting Series. However, Getty-Dubay Italic Calligraphy is also an excellent stand-alone introduction to italic letterforms. The last worksheet in the book, Cursive Italic, may also be done with a pencil or regular pen. Teachers tell me that this is the point when students get excited about applying what they've learned to their own day-to-day handwriting.

> *"It slows down my body."*
> Adam
>
> *"It's very flowing and beautiful."*
> Lucia
>
> *"When you get the rhythm it's really calming and feels like an ocean flowing."*
> Georgia
>
> *"It makes me feel calm and like I'm in a place like Hawaii. When I'm doing the serifs it makes me feel good."*
> Josiah
>
> Second graders, ACCESS Academy,
> Portland Public Schools,
> when asked individually what they like about calligraphy

In the introductory pages, teachers and at-home learners will find how to select the necessary materials for the study of calligraphy, to be aware of the mechanics of writing, to manage the classroom for optimum learning and practice, to use the historical charts and to practice with cards and letters, to use relevant vocabulary, and to access videos and do-it-yourself (DIY) worksheets.

Please bear these simple principles in mind:

The learning process is both kinesthetic and contextual. The student learns the shapes by tracing progressively fainter letter shapes (black, gray, pen angle lines, solid outlines, and dotted outlines). This process creates muscle memory.

Tracing is a rehearsal and copying is a performance. The student first traces letterforms, then copies them. After that, the student can use letters contextually by writing pangrams, poems, quotes, and other words of their choosing.

The secret for success in calligraphy is maintaining the correct pen angle. The correct pen edge angle for lowercase letters is 45º (a flatter pen angle for s, z, and crossbars of f and t), while the pen angle for capital letters is 15º (steeper for N).

Let your students savor the "adagio" experience of italic calligraphy. Adagio means a slow and easy tempo in Italian—so applicable to the practice of calligraphy! It reminds me of a road sign on the campus of Reed College, in Portland, Oregon. Instead of the stern command: "SLOW," the sign suggests: "Slow Down. Observe & Enjoy."

Slow down, enjoy the process of calligraphy, and fall in love with letters along the way!

Inga Dubay
Portland, Oregon
August, 2016

THE EDGED PEN & OTHER MATERIALS

Edged pen
There are three types of edged pen: Fiber-tip pen, cartridge pen, and dip pen. Choose nib widths as close as possible to 3.5mm and 2mm.

- FIBER-TIP PEN options:
  Staedtler Duo with 3.5mm and 2mm on either end (black, red, purple, blue, green).
  Marvy Uchida Calligraphy with 3.5mm and 2mm on either end (24 colors).
  Marvy single nib pen 3.5mm and Marvy single nib pen 2mm.

- CARTRIDGE PEN options:
  Pilot Parallel pen with 3.8mm and 2mm nib.
  Sheaffer cartridge pen with 2mm nib (Broad).

- DIP PEN options for nibs and holders:
  Dip pen nibs – Speedball C-2 for 3.5mm; Speedball C-4 for 2mm.
  Dip pen holder – Speedball, or other brands.

Holder option: Make your own nib holder with a dowel and tubing. Use ¼" wood dowel sawed to 6" length; and ¼" (inside measurement) clear flexible tubing cut with scissors to 2½" length. Fit the dowel into the tubing and slip the nib between the dowel and the tubing. For a double-edged pen, place flexible tubing on both ends of the dowel and place a 3.5mm nib on one end and a 2mm nib on the other end. (Dowels and tubing are available at hardware stores.)

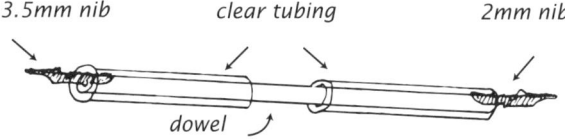

Ink
Only use non-waterproof ink, such as Higgins Eternal. To avoid spilling ink, place the bottle in a tuna can or a similar size container, or cut an X with a utility knife into a plastic top, then slip this top over the ink bottle.

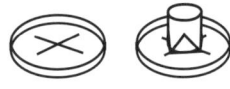

Use a cotton rag to wipe the pen nib dry at the end of the writing session.

Care of pens and ink: When writing is finished, re-cap fiber-tip or cartridge pens, or wipe dry the ink nibs. Re-cap ink containers.

Care of fiber-tip pens: Be sure to keep pens capped when not in use as the ink can dry out quickly. If too much pressure is placed on the nibs, they will lose their crisp edge and become blunt. Often when this happens, pens are thrown away. However, they can be salvaged in the following ways:

- If fiber-tip pens run dry and the nibs are still crisp, they can be used as dip pens with non-waterproof ink available in bottles.

- If fiber-tip pens become blunt and lose their edge, use an X-Acto knife to sharpen the edge. However, if the ink is dried out and the nib is blunt, there is no remedy. Discard.

Book
13 Introductory pages.
20 Worksheets (3.5 mm nib).
9 Worksheets (2mm nib).
8 Historical Charts (lowercase).
9 Historical Charts (capitals).
5 Ruled lines may be copied for student use.

Pencil
Use a pencil for writing the date, drawing a star to mark one's personal best letter, underlining a letter that needs extra work, and for tracing monoline capitals.

Practice Paper
Use any paper that does not allow ink to bleed through. Recommended: 25% rag paper, which is a treat to write on!

Second paper/following paper
Place a second piece of paper on top of the worksheet below the line of writing. This will protect the page from moisture or oil from the writing hand and from any possible errant ink spots. It also helps focus attention on the actual writing line.

Easel (optional)
An easel is helpful in providing a slanted writing surface. Foam core is a good material to use. Cut two pieces 12" x 12" that are 3/16" thick and tape them together at one edge.

Use a plastic cup, book, block of wood, etc., to prop open to any desired slant for writing.

Making larger-sized letters: Tape two pencils together by holding them side-by-side and placing tape around them at the eraser end and also near the pencil tip, at the paint edge. For writing on a blackboard, tape two pieces of chalk together. For writing on a whiteboard, tape two dry erase pens together. If a wider letter is needed, place a spacer between the writing tools.

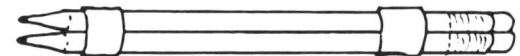

© 2016 Getty-Dubay

MECHANICS

Correct pen hold for both left-handed and right-handed people
Hold the pen between the thumb and index finger, resting it on your middle finger. Be sure the tip of the thumb touches the pen. Rest the shaft of the pen near the large knuckle. Avoid a death grip or thumb wrap!

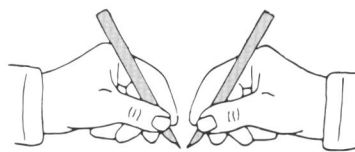

Alternative pen hold
Hold the pen between the index finger and the middle finger, resting it by the large knuckles. Tip of thumb touches the pen. Hold in the standard way at the tips of the fingers. This hold is comfortable for some. This hold avoids a death grip or thumb wrap.

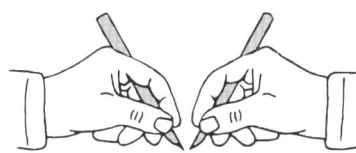

Paper position
Right-handed: Hold the book straight, try not to tip right or left. Use the non-writing hand to hold the book.

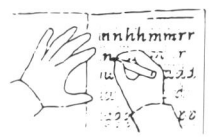

Left-handed: Turn book clockwise so top of book is parallel to the right side of the desk. Use the non-writing hand to hold the book.

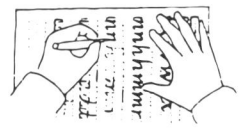

When writing on the left side of the book (even numbered pages), bend the book over the edge of the desk.

How to sit
Sit up straight with feet on the floor.

FLAT SURFACE   SLANTED SURFACE

Letter slope and pen angle: All letters and numerals in the worksheets are written with a 5° slope. Use a 45° pen angle for lowercase (slightly flatter angle for s, z, crossbars of f and t) and a 15° pen angle for capitals and numerals (45° pen angle for N).

EXPERIMENTING WITH THE EDGED PEN

> *"Prepare your eye, prepare your hand."*
> Deborah Davis,
> University of Chicago Laboratory School.

As an optional introduction to the edged pen before starting the worksheets in this book, explore the possibilities of the edged pen.

Clear desk of all clutter. Allow hand and arm to move as needed. Non-writing hand holds paper.

Materials needed: Edged pen (fiber-tip pen, cartridge pen, or dip pen and ink), blank paper 8.5" x 11" or larger.

⬥ What are some ways to write the **thickest** line possible with an edged pen?

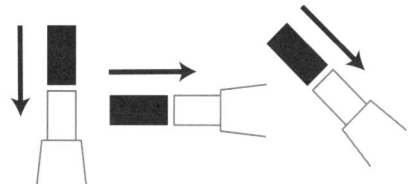

(Place pen nib horizontally and pull pen down. Place pen nib vertically and pull horizontally. Place pen nib diagonally and pull diagonally.)

⬥ What are some ways to write the **thinnest** line possible with an edged pen?

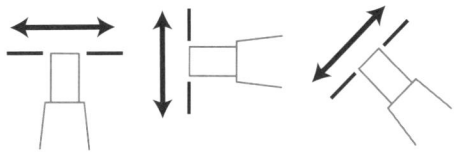

(Place pen nib horizontally and move horizontally in either direction. Place pen nib vertically and move down or up. Place pen nib diagonally and move diagonally.)

⬥ What other interesting marks can the edged pen make?

⬥ Notice what happens with your elbow when you change pen position.

At end of session, recap pen or wipe pen nib dry with cotton cloth and recap ink container.

(Option: These exercises can also be done on larger paper using a foam brush with a width of 1" or more.)

CLASSROOM MANAGEMENT

Allow one session per week of about 30 minutes. If possible, twice a week. Include Historical Chart if time allows. Use one worksheet per session.

Provide a place for students to store books. Organize all materials in a storage container that provides easy access for students. Direct students to clear their workspace of all clutter and distractions.

Distribute materials:
- book
- fiber-tip pen, cartridge pen, or dip pen with ink container & cotton rag
- a second sheet to place under writing hand
- pencil

Direct instruction

1. Direct students to leave pens capped or ink containers capped and book closed until the time to write (#7).

2. Begin with warm-up exercises for hands: rub hands together, shake hands up, down and sideways to get oxygen into the fingers. Finger dexterity and light touch exercise: thumb to index finger, thumb to middle finger, thumb to ring finger, thumb to little finger, then backwards, then faster, then slower.

3. Have students stand up to write large letters in the air using the correct stroke sequence. (Present letters on the session's worksheet.) Say aloud and have students repeat: "All letters start at the top, except lowercase d."

4. Demonstrate the correct pen hold and direct students to hold pen without a "death grip" or thumb wrap. (See Mechanics.) For a lighter touch, tap first finger three times on pen.

5. Demonstrate letters using a document reader and/or show Instructional Video (see p. 9). Demonstrate the correct pen angle on the square at the left side of writing line, then trace over the letters showing the correct stroke sequence. Review objectives shown at the top of the page. (See Glossary.) Remember you do not have to be an expert; you are modeling learning as you demonstrate!

6. Demonstrate correct book positions for both right-handed and left-handed students (see p. 7).

7. Direct students to uncap pens, or uncap ink containers, and open the book to begin writing. Place a second sheet of paper under the writing hand just below the line of writing to protect the page and to help focus on the line of writing. The non-writing hand holds book in place.

8. Direct students to check their pen angle by lining up the pen with the angle within the square at the beginning of every writing line. Getting the correct pen angle is the secret to success in calligraphy! For every solid black image, direct students to trace with the pen just above the image, not touching the paper. Then, put pen to paper for the next images (gray, dashed, outlined, and dotted outline).

9. Circulate through the room. Advise students to slow down and not hurry. As much as possible, comment on correct book position (especially left-handers), pen hold, pen angle, and stroke sequence.

10. Just before the end of the session, direct students to do Self-Evaluation: LOOK, PLAN, PRACTICE (located at the bottom of each student worksheet).

    LOOK: Direct students to find their own personal best correct pen angle or best letter and to give that letter a star.
    PLAN: Direct students to find a letter whose pen angle or shape could be improved, underline it and then plan how that letter shape or pen angle could be improved.
    PRACTICE: Direct students to write the improved letter in a free space on the page.
    Optional: If time allows, share accomplishment of best letter with neighbor and tell why that letter was chosen.

11. Direct students to recap pen so ink doesn't dry out or wipe the dip pen dry and recap ink container. Close book when ink is dry and store in designated area. Return all calligraphy materials to the storage container.

12. Congratulate all students on their calligraphic accomplishments of the day!

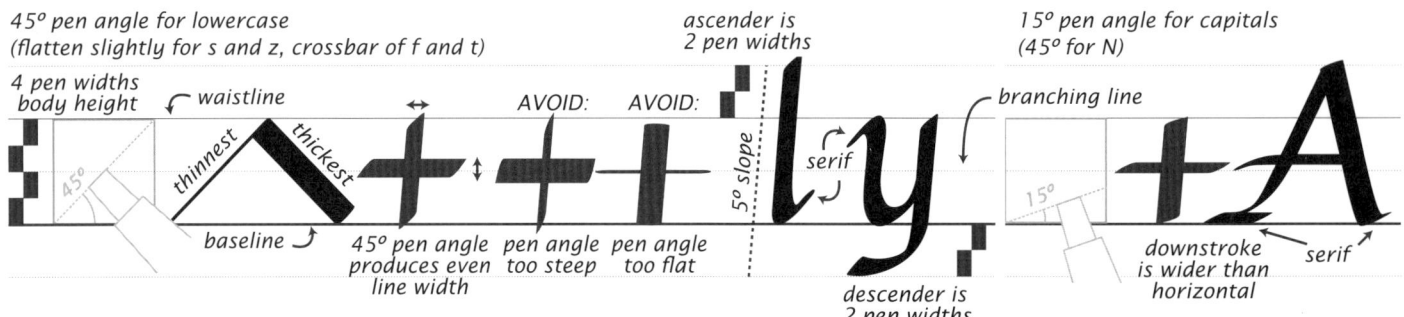

SUPPLEMENTARY MATERIALS

Instructional videos, do-it-yourself worksheets, and a Certificate of Completion are available to owners of Getty-Dubay Italic Calligraphy: for School & Home. Access them by visiting:

www.handwritingsuccess.com

VIDEOS: Inga Dubay demonstrates lowercase and formal capitals for worksheets using a 3.5mm nib. Use them as part of classroom instruction, for independent study or teacher development.

DIY WORKSHEETS: Make your own worksheets online and print them out for extra practice. Text that you enter will appear in the Getty-Dubay Italic Calligraphy font on every other line, ready for tracing and copying. Select 3.5mm or 2mm pen nib size and style of letter.

CERTIFICATE OF COMPLETION: To acknowledge the accomplishment of completing this book, print out a personalized certificate.

THE GOLDEN RATIO

The golden ratio has held a special fascination since antiquity. The ratio of long-to-short sides based on the golden number, known as Phi, is frequently found in art, architecture, and even in nature. It is mentioned in Euclid's Elements (ca. 300 BCE) and was known to artists and philosophers, such as Leonardo Da Vinci.

A rectangle based on the golden ratio has the property that when a square is removed, a smaller rectangle of the same proportion remains. A smaller square can be removed again, and so on, with a spiral pattern resulting, similar to that of a nautilus shell. (An arc described in each square forms a spiral.)

The golden ratio's mathematical source is the Fibonacci Series: 0, 1, 1, 2, 3, 5, 8, 13, 21, 34, 55, 89, etc. As the numbers in the series grow, the ratio of two consecutive numbers approaches Phi, approximately 1.618. A golden rectangle has side lengths in the proportion of the golden ratio (for example 5 x 8 or 21 x 34).

How to construct a golden rectangle: Begin with a square; draw a diagonal (AB) of half of the square; the length of half the square (AC) plus the diagonal (AB) is equal to the length of a golden rectangle (AB + AC = CD).

For a visual demonstration, see Walt Disney's movie, Donald [Duck] in Mathmagic Land.

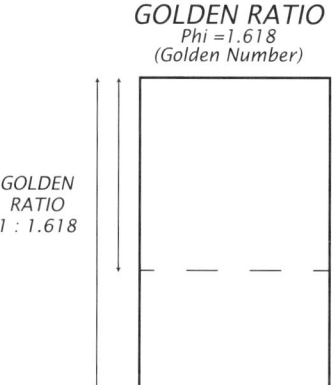

GOLDEN RATIO
Phi = 1.618
(Golden Number)

GOLDEN RATIO
1 : 1.618

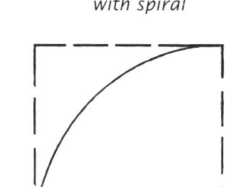

GOLDEN RECTANGLE
with spiral

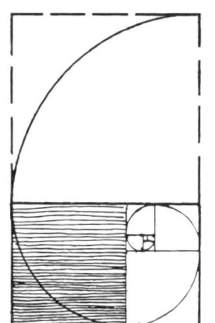

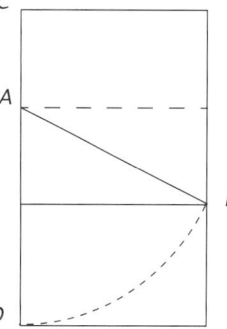

DRAW A GOLDEN RECTANGLE

Italic letter shapes are based on the golden ratio:

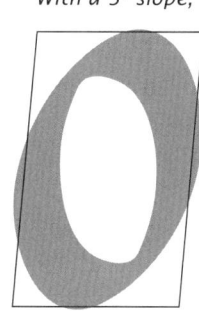

With a 5° slope, the golden rectangle becomes a "golden parallelogram."

© 2016 Getty-Dubay

HISTORICAL CHARTS

A window into the wondrous story of the history of letters.

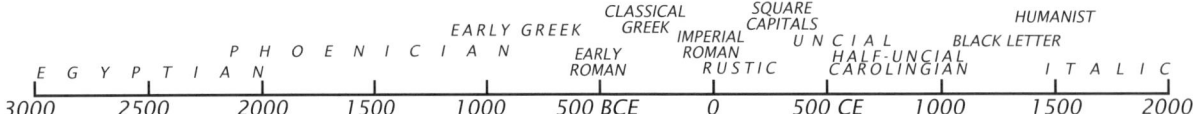

It all began in about 3,000 BCE. In fact, the history of our alphabet parallels the history of Western civilization. As the historical diagrams in this book illustrate, the Egyptians were among the first to pick up a brush or pen to communicate. And from the land of the pyramids and hieroglyphs we go forward in time to Greece, Rome, and Europe. We finally reach our modern-day italic letterforms. Those letterforms, which we use today for our handwriting, gradually transformed as they made their way from the Roman Era, through the Renaissance, and on to the present.

On the worksheets for Formal Capitals, you will find how capital letters developed in the writing of Egyptians, Phoenicians, Early Greeks, Classical Greeks, and Romans. The worksheets and the historical charts go hand-in-hand; the charts are on the left-hand pages of the book and the worksheets are on the right. The first eight charts show the development of lowercase letters. Following them are nine charts showing the development of capital letters.

Lowercase letters developed gradually from Roman capitals. Some are a shorthand version of the capital (R r) while others are a smaller version (S s). Notice that there is no differentiation between capital and lowercase letters for three styles of pen-written letters of the Roman Era, namely, Square Capitals, Rustic Capitals and Uncial Capitals. Lowercase letters didn't appear in those styles until the fifth century.

Another fun fact: The alphabet in general did not start out with twenty-six letters but evolved over the centuries. For example, J, U, and W did not exist in the Roman alphabet. J didn't appear until the twelfth century, and back then was used as a long i. J didn't stand alone as a member of our alphabet until the sixteenth century. Likewise, W was a later addition, joining the alphabet in the eleventh century. And U followed a long and winding road, starting out as a V in the Latin alphabet, acquiring its U shape in the Uncial style of writing, and finally becoming part of the alphabet in the sixteenth century.

Source: Berthold L. Ullman, *Ancient Writing and Its Influence*. New York: Longmans, Green & Co., 1932.

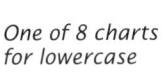

One of 8 charts for lowercase

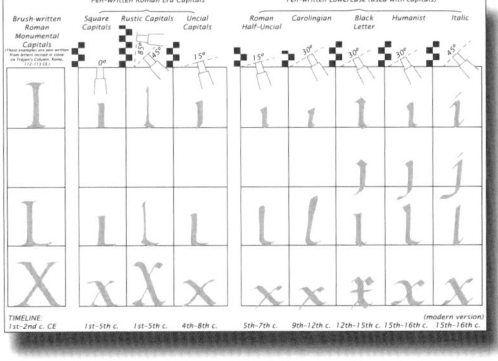

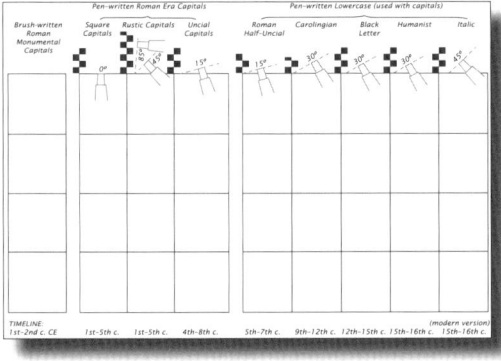

Ruled lines for lowercase page 60

One of 9 charts for capitals

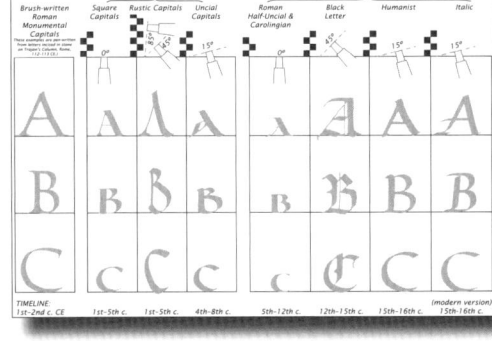

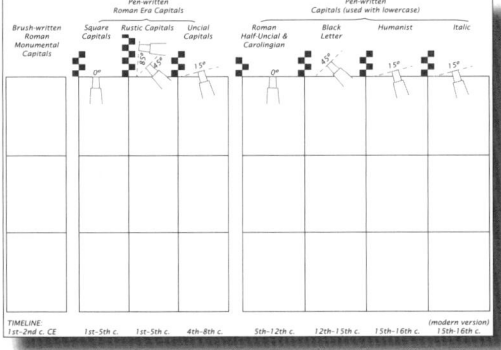

Ruled lines for capitals page 62

These historical charts may be used in two ways:

EYES ONLY: The student notices the letter shape and size changes occuring during the development from Roman times to present day. The student notices how the letter shapes change from the brush-written/incised letters to the pen-written letters.

EYES & HANDS-ON: After the EYES ONLY exercise, the student uses the ruled lines for the Historical Charts (pages 60 & 62) to copy the letters by figuring out the stroke sequence of each letter. (Hint: top to bottom, left to right.)

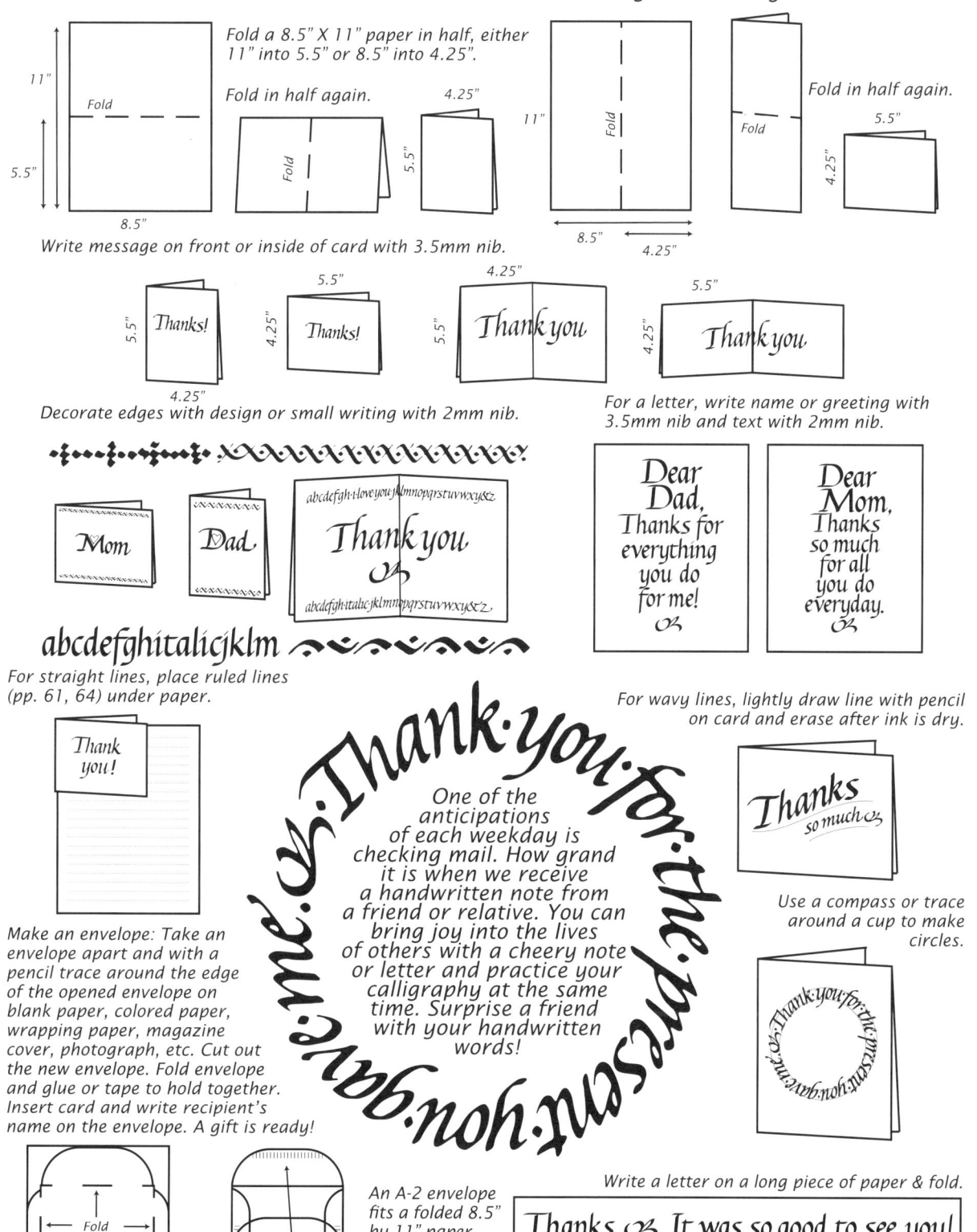

VARIATIONS & IMPROVISATIONS

The process of learning italic calligraphy begins with developing basic skills. However, your own italic calligraphy is unique. Variations and improvisation are part of the art. After you learn the basics, explore variations and sing your own song!

In this book, the basics are a 5° slope for letters and four pen widths for the body height (x-height) of the letters. Basic skills include manipulating the pen at the correct pen angle and maintaining a consistent pen angle as well as knowing the correct letterforms and stroke sequences. Practice the letterforms until they are "in your hand." Then variations can be explored.

When you begin to make variations and improvise, one time you may choose to change the slope of the letters and another time the height. Yet another choice might be to change both slope and height. Explore!

CAUTION: Whatever variation you choose, BE CONSISTENT. If it's a 0° pen angle and 5 pen widths high, keep to those chosen variations when writing a quote, poem, or prose. Then try another variation for a different look. Notice what slope and/or letter size seems more comfortable. Some choices will be motivated by the eye and some by the hand.

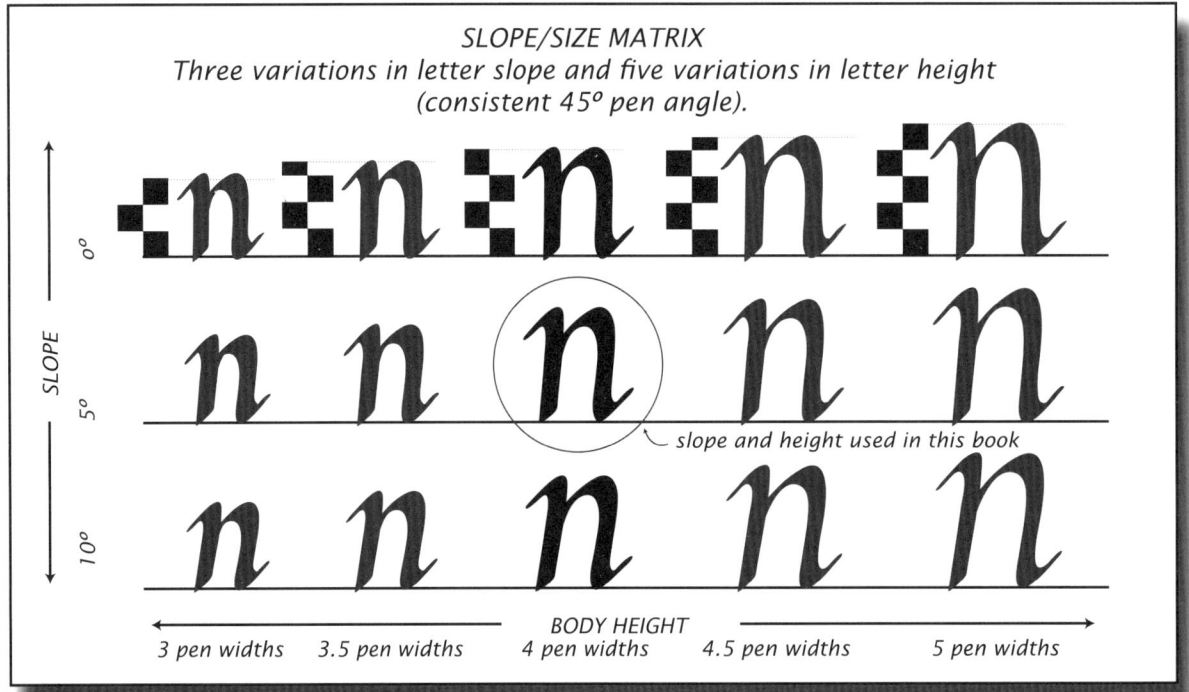

Other possible variations: a steeper pen angle creates narrower letters; a flatter pen angle creates wider letters.

PEN PLAY

GLOSSARY

Angular chin: The shape of a d g q at the baseline and the shape of b p at the waistline.
Arch shape: Counter shape formed when branching out, as in letters n h m r (Lowercase Family 3).
Ascender: The part of a lowercase letter that extends above the body height.
Ascender line/Capital height line: Lowercase ascenders b d f h k l touch this line, as do all capitals.
Baseline: The line upon which letters sit; bottom of body height.
Basic a shape: Counter shape formed in letters a d g q (Lowercase Family 5).
Body height: The distance between the baseline and waistline, or x-height.
Branching line: A line at the center of the x-height where branching out occurs in n h m r b p and branching in occurs in u y a d g q.
Calligraphy: Beautiful or elegant writing using an edged pen or brush.
Capital letter: A letter in a series A B C rather than a b c. Also called uppercase, large letter, majuscule, or caps (plural).
Counter: The open area within a letter.
Crossbar: A horizontal line crossing the downstroke at the waistline, as in letters f t (Lowercase Family 8).
Descender: The part of a lowercase letter that extends below the baseline.
Descender line: Lowercase descenders f g j p q y touch this line. (Same line as ascender/capital line for the next line of writing.)
Diagonal: A line from upper right to lower left or lower left to upper right, as in letters k v w x z (Lowercase Family 2).
Downstroke: A line from top to bottom following letter slope angle, as in letters i l j (Lowercase Family 1).
Elliptical: Counter shape formed by compressing a circular shape, as in letters o e c (Lowercase Family 7).
Elliptical curve: A curved line, as in letter o, the left side of a d g q e c, and the right side of b p.
Exterior triangular counter: The left side at the waistline of n h m r b p; right side at the baseline of a d g q u y.
Fibonacci Series: 0, 1, 1, 2, 3. 5, 8, 13, 21, 34, 55, 89, etc. where each number is the sum of the two previous numbers.
Flourish: An extra stroke added to a letter or serif.
Golden ratio: Two measurements whose proportion is "Phi" (approximately 1.618).
Golden rectangle: A rectangle whose lengths are in the golden ratio. With a 5º slope, it becomes a "golden parallelogram." The italic lowercase lettters that fit in a golden rectangle are a c e n o s u v x z.

Horizontal: A line extending from left to right parallel to the baseline and waistline.
Horizontal entrance and exit serif: The serif is written from left to right.
Inverted a shape: Counter shape formed when branching out, as in letters b p (Lowercase Family 6).
Inverted arch shape: Counter shape formed when branching in, as in letters u y (Lowercase Family 4).
Letter shape: The correct form of a capital or lowercase letter.
Letter size: The height or length of a letter.
Letter slope: The consistent slope of letters. (5º slope of italic calligraphy in this book.)
Letter spacing: The distance between letters in a word.
Letter speed: The rate of writing.
Letter strokes: The lines without lifts used to write a letter (one-stroke, two-stroke, etc.).
Ligature: A character formed by connecting two letters into a single form.
Lowercase letter: A letter in a series a b c rather than A B C. Also called small letter, minuscule.
Pangram: A sentence that contains all the letters of the alphabet.
Pen edge angle (p.a.): The angle of the edge of the pen nib in relation to the base line, referred to as pen angle. (The word "pen" is from the Latin penna, "feather." An edged pen produces thick and thin strokes through a constant pen angle.)
Pen width: The measurement of the pen nib, as in 3.5mm or 2mm.
Sans serif, sans-serif: From French word sans, "without" serifs or without any additions to the letter.
Serif: An entrance stroke or exit stroke.
Sharp angle entrance serif: The serif enters lowercase letter at 45º with a sharp angle (only j and p).
Sharp angle exit serif: The serif exits at 45º on lowercase q, 15º on some capitals.
Soft angle entrance serif: The serif enters lowercase letter at 45º with a soft angle.
Soft angle exit serif: The serif exits lowercase letter at 45º with a soft angle.
Spacing: The "pleasing" adjustment of letter to letter, word to word, line to line.
Triangular counter: The shape formed by serifs at the baseline and at the top of capitals, also the shape formed by diagonals.
Vertical: A line from top to bottom following the slope line.
Waistline: The top of body height or x-height, top of lowercase letters without ascenders.
Word spacing: The distance between words in a sentence (width of an n).

DEVELOPMENT OF LOWERCASE FAMILY 1 (i l j x) and FAMILY 2 (x only)

Brush-written Roman Monumental Capitals (These examples are pen-written from letters incised in stone on Trajan's Column, Rome, 112–113 CE.)	Pen-written Roman Era Capitals			Pen-written Lowercase (used with capitals)				
	Square Capitals	Rustic Capitals	Uncial Capitals	Roman Half-Uncial	Carolingian	Black Letter	Humanist	Italic
	0°	85° / 45°	15°	15°	30°	30°	30°	45°

TIMELINE: 1st–2nd c. CE | 1st–5th c. | 1st–5th c. | 4th–8th c. | 5th–7th c. | 9th–12th c. | 12th–15th c. | 15th–16th c. | 15th–16th c. (modern version)

© 2016 Getty-Dubay

LOWERCASE FAMILY 1 (i l j) and FAMILY 2 (x only)

OBJECTIVES: 45° pen angle, 5° slope. Family 1 – Straight line downstroke. **Downstroke** – top to bottom.
Ascender – l. **Descender** – j.
Serifs: **soft angle entrance serif** – i, **soft angle exit serif** – i and l, **sharp angle entrance serif** – j.
One-stroke – l, **two-stroke** – i j.
Trace with pen just above solid black letters (almost touching); touch pen to paper for all other letters.

Hint: Breathe out on downstroke for a straighter line.

"xi": a Greek letter

LOOK, PLAN, PRACTICE: Look for your personal best pen angle or best letter. Give yourself a star! Now, find a letter that you could improve. **Plan** how to improve—is it the pen angle or the letter shape? **Practice** the improved letter by writing it in a free space on the page.

© 2016 Getty-Dubay

DEVELOPMENT OF LOWERCASE FAMILY 2 (k v w z) See x, p. 14

Date _____

	Brush-written Roman Monumental Capitals	Pen-written Roman Era Capitals			Pen-written Lowercase (used with capitals)				
		Square Capitals (0°)	Rustic Capitals (85°/45°)	Uncial Capitals (15°)	Roman Half-Uncial (15°)	Carolingian (30°)	Black Letter (30°)	Humanist (30°)	Italic (45°)
K	K (rarely used)	K	K K	K	k k	k k	k	k k	k k k
V	V	v v	V V	u	u u	u u	v	v v	v v
W							w w	w w w	w w
Z	Z *Greek letter zeta added 1st c. BCE*		1	Z Z	Z Z Z				Z Z Z

TIMELINE: 1st–2nd c. CE | 1st–5th c. | 1st–5th c. | 4th–8th c. | 5th–7th c. | 9th–12th c. | 12th–15th c. | 15th–16th c. | 15th–16th c. (modern version)

16

© 2016 Getty-Dubay

LOWERCASE FAMILY 2 (k v w x z)

OBJECTIVES: *45° pen angle, 5° slope.* Flatten pen angle slightly for z (ca. 30°). Review Family 1 and x of Family 2.
Family 2 – Diagonal line. Counter – triangular shape. **Ascender** – k.
Serifs: **soft angle entrance serif** – v w x, **soft angle exit serif** – k x, **sharp angle entrance serif** – 2nd stroke of k,
sharp angle exit serif – v w, **horizontal entrance and exit serif** – 2nd stroke of x.
One-stroke – k v w z, **two-stroke** – k x. (Option: one or two-stroke k.)
Trace with pen just above solid black letters (almost touching); touch pen to paper for all other letters.

45° pen angle

1

REVIEW

ilj · ilj · ilj · jill · xi

2

NEW

l k k k k or k k k k k

3

v v v v w w w w

4

flatten pen angle slightly for z

x x x x z z z z

5

k or k v w x z k v w x z

6

kiwi · kiwi · kiwi

7

will · will · will

8

LOOK, PLAN, PRACTICE: **Look** for your personal best pen angle or best letter. Give yourself a star! Now, find a letter that you could improve.
Plan how to improve—is it the pen angle or the letter shape? **Practice** the improved letter by writing it in a free space on the page.

© 2016 Getty-Dubay

DEVELOPMENT OF LOWERCASE FAMILY 3 (n m h r)

Date _____

Brush-written Roman Monumental Capitals (These examples are pen-written from letters incised in stone on Trajan's Column, Rome, 112–113 CE.)	Pen-written Roman Era Capitals			Pen-written Lowercase (used with capitals)				
	Square Capitals 0°	Rustic Capitals 85°/45°	Uncial Capitals 15°	Roman Half-Uncial 15°	Carolingian 30°	Black Letter 30°	Humanist 30°	Italic 45°
N	N	N	N	N	n	n	n	n
M	M	M	M	m	m	m	m	m
H	H	H	h	h	h	h	h	h
R	R	R	R	r	r	r	r	r

TIMELINE: 1st–2nd c. CE 1st–5th c. 1st–5th c. 4th–8th c. 5th–7th c. 9th–12th c. 12th–15th c. 15th–16th c. 15th–16th c. (modern version)

© 2016 Getty-Dubay

LOWERCASE FAMILY 3 (n h m r)

OBJECTIVES: 45° pen angle, 5° slope. Flatten pen angle slightly for z (ca. 30°). Review Family 1 and 2.
Family 3 – Arch. Counter – arch shape. **Branching line –** branching out at center of x-height n h m r. **Exterior triangular counter** at waistline. **Ascender –** h. Serifs: **soft angle entrance serif –** n m r, **soft angle exit serif –** n h m.
One-stroke – n h m r.
Trace with pen just above solid black letters (almost touching); touch pen to paper for all other letters.

Turkish finger cymbal

LOOK, PLAN, PRACTICE: Look for your personal best pen angle or best letter. Give yourself a star! Now, find a letter that you could improve. **Plan** how to improve—is it the pen angle or the letter shape? **Practice** the improved letter by writing it in a free space on the page.

© 2016 Getty-Dubay

DEVELOPMENT OF LOWERCASE Family 4 (u y)

Pen-written Roman Era Capitals

Brush-written Roman Monumental Capitals	Square Capitals	Rustic Capitals	Uncial Capitals
(These examples are pen-written from letters incised in stone on Trajan's Column, Rome, 112–113 CE.)	0°	85° / 45°	15°
Greek letter upsilon added 1st c. BCE — Y	Y	Y	U / Y

Pen-written Lowercase (used with capitals)

Roman Half-Uncial	Carolingian	Black Letter	Humanist	Italic
15°	30°	30°	30°	45°
u / y	u / y	u / y	u / y	u / y *(modern version)*

TIMELINE:
1st–2nd c. CE   1st–5th c.   1st–5th c.   4th–8th c.   5th–7th c.   9th–12th c.   12th–15th c.   15th–16th c.   15th–16th c.

Date _____

20

© 2016 Getty-Dubay

LOWERCASE FAMILY 4 (u y)

OBJECTIVES: 45° pen angle, 5° slope. Flatten pen angle slightly for z (ca. 30°). Review Family 1 to 3.
Family 4 – Inverted arch. Counter – inverted arch shape. **Branching line –** branching in at center of x-height u y. **Exterior triangular counter** at baseline. **Descender –** y.
Serifs: soft angle entrance serif – u y. **One-stroke –** u y. Optional two-stroke y based on v shape.
Trace with pen just above solid black letters (almost touching); touch pen to paper for all other letters.

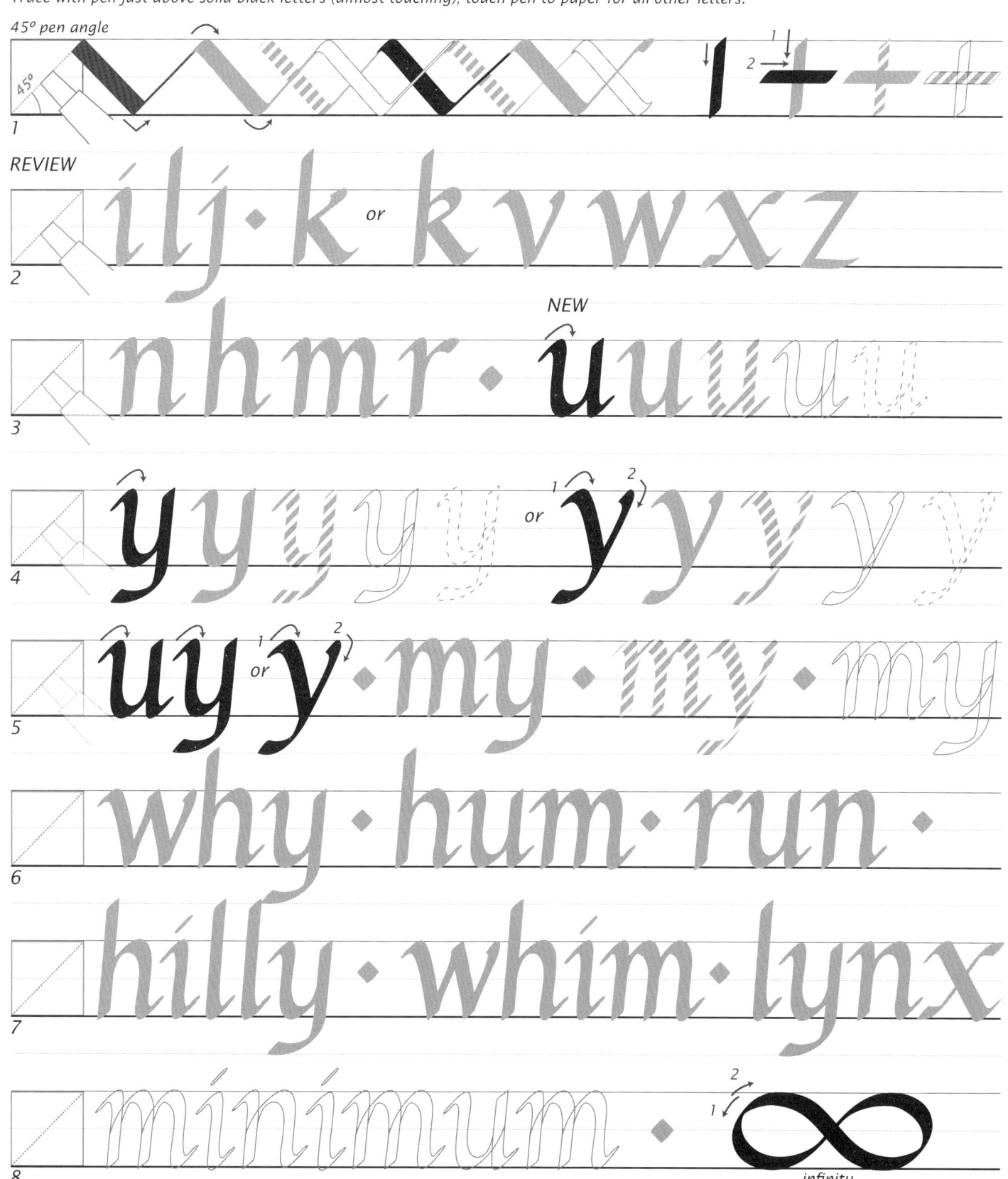

LOOK, PLAN, PRACTICE: **Look** for your personal best pen angle or best letter. Give yourself a star! Now, find a letter that you could improve.
Plan how to improve—is it the pen angle or the letter shape? **Practice** the improved letter by writing it in a free space on the page.

© 2016 Getty-Dubay

DEVELOPMENT OF LOWERCASE FAMILY 5 (a d g q)

_____ Date

Brush-written Roman Monumental Capitals (These examples are pen-written from letters incised in stone on Trajan's Column, Rome, 112–113 CE.)	Pen-written Roman Era Capitals			Pen-written Lowercase (used with capitals)				
	Square Capitals 0°	Rustic Capitals 85°/45°	Uncial Capitals 15°	Roman Half-Uncial 15°	Carolingian 30°	Black Letter 30°	Humanist 30°	Italic 45°
A	A	A	A	a	a	a	a	a
D	D	D	D	d	d	d	d	d
G	G	G	G	ʒ	g	g	g	g
Q	Q	Q	q	q	q	q	q	q

TIMELINE: 1st–2nd c. CE   1st–5th c.   1st–5th c.   4th–8th c.   5th–7th c.   9th–11th c.   12th–15th c.   15th–16th c.   15th–16th c. (modern version)

© 2016 Getty-Dubay

LOWERCASE FAMILY 5 (a d g q)

OBJECTIVES: 45° pen angle, 5° slope. Flatten pen angle slightly for z (ca. 30°). Review Family 1 to 4.
Family 5 – Basic a shape. **Counter** – basic a shape. **Elliptical curve** left side, **angular chin** at baseline. Branching in halfway between baseline and waistline. **Exterior triangular counter** at baseline.
Ascender – d. **Descender** – g q. Serifs: **soft angle exit serif** – a d, **sharp angle exit serif** – q.
One-stroke – a d g q. Note: All lowercase letters start at the top except d.
Trace with pen just above solid black letters (almost touching); touch pen to paper for all other letters.

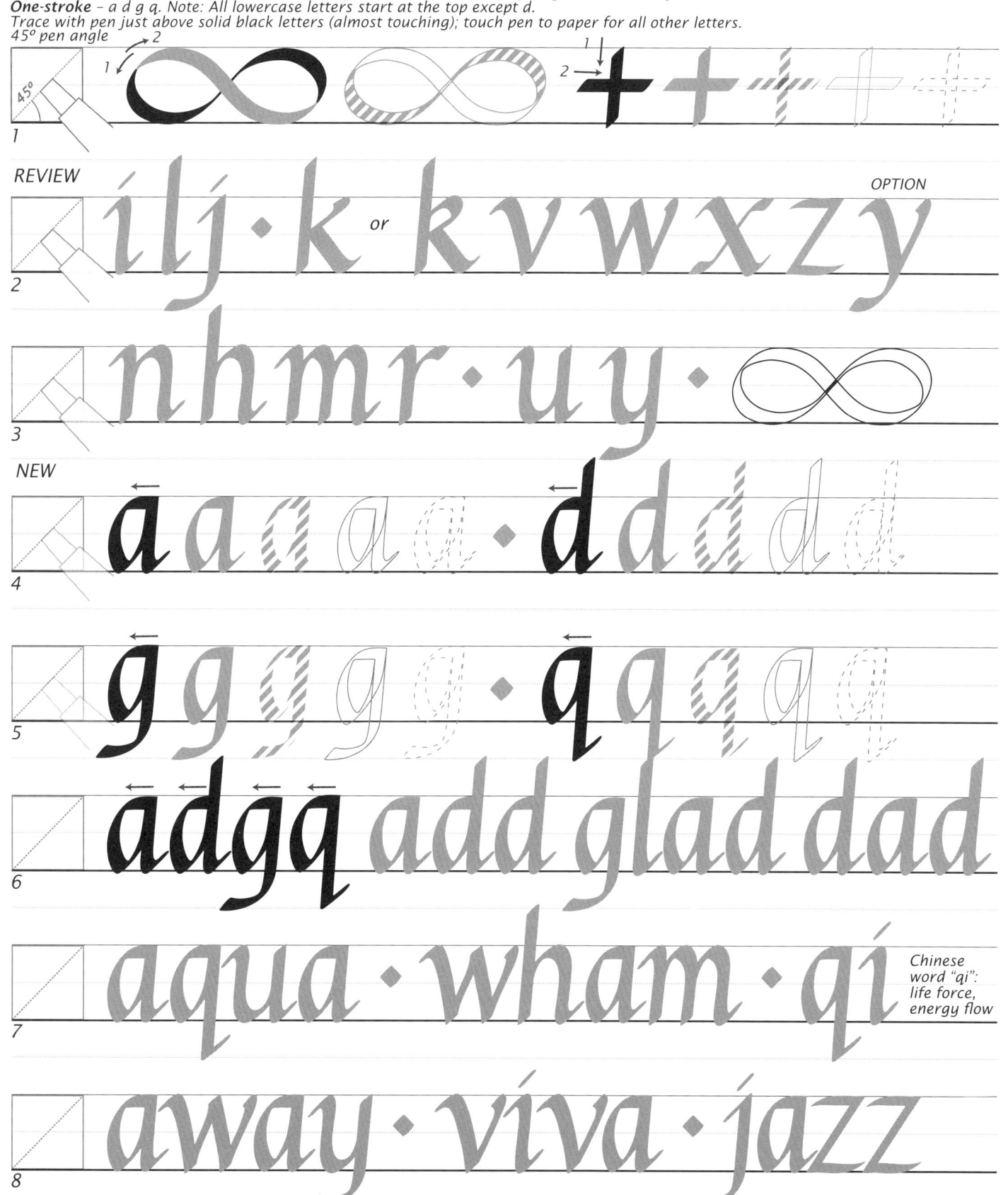

LOOK, PLAN, PRACTICE: **Look** for your personal best pen angle or best letter. Give yourself a star! Now, find a letter that you could improve.
Plan how to improve—is it the pen angle or the letter shape? **Practice** the improved letter by writing it in a free space on the page.

© 2016 Getty-Dubay

DEVELOPMENT OF LOWERCASE FAMILY 6 (*b p*)

_____ Date

Brush-written Roman Monumental Capitals (These examples are pen-written from letters incised in stone on Trajan's Column, Rome, 112–113 CE.)	Pen-written Roman Era Capitals			Pen-written Lowercase (used with capitals)				
	Square Capitals 0°	Rustic Capitals 85° / 45°	Uncial Capitals 15°	Roman Half-Uncial 15°	Carolingian 30°	Black Letter 30°	Humanist 30°	Italic 45°
B	B	B	B	b	b	b	b	b
P	P	P	P	p	p	p	p	p

TIMELINE: 1st–2nd c. CE   1st–5th c.   1st–5th c.   4th–8th c.   5th–7th c.   9th–12th c.   12th–15th c.   15th–16th c.   15th–16th c. *(modern version)*

© 2016 Getty-Dubay

LOWERCASE FAMILY 6 (b p)

OBJECTIVES: 45° pen angle, 5° slope. Flatten pen angle slightly for z (ca. 30°). Review Family 1 to 5.
Family 6 – inverted basic a shape. **Counter** – inverted basic a shape. **Elliptical curve** right side. Branching out halfway between baseline and waistline. **Angular chin** at waistline. **Exterior triangular counter** at waistline. **Ascender** – b. **Descender** – p.
Serifs: **sharp angle entrance serif** – p. **One-stroke** – b p.
Trace with pen just above solid black letters (almost touching); touch pen to paper for all other letters.

45° pen angle

1.

REVIEW   OPTION

2. ilj · k   or   k v w x z y ·

3. nhmr · uy · adgq

NEW

4. bbbbb   ppppp   bp

5. bump · pip · bib ·

6. baby · puppy · paw

7. jib · jump · zap ·

"Cosmic flower," Lloyd Reynolds

8. pax · pumpkin

LOOK, PLAN, PRACTICE: Look for your personal best pen angle or best letter. Give yourself a star! Now, find a letter that you could improve.
Plan how to improve—is it the pen angle or the letter shape? **Practice** the improved letter by writing it in a free space on the page.

© 2016 Getty-Dubay

DEVELOPMENT OF LOWERCASE FAMILY 7 (o e c s)

Brush-written Roman Monumental Capitals	Pen-written Roman Era Capitals			Pen-written Lowercase (used with capitals)				
(These examples are pen-written from letters incised in stone on Trajan's Column, Rome, 112–113 CE.)	Square Capitals 0°	Rustic Capitals 85°/45°	Uncial Capitals 15°	Roman Half-Uncial 15°	Carolingian 30°	Black Letter 30°	Humanist 30°	Italic 45°
O	O	O	O	O	O	O	O	O
E	E	E	E	E	e	e	e	e
C	C	C	C	C	C	C	C	C
S	S	S	S	S	S	S	S	S

TIMELINE: 1st–2nd c. CE   1st–5th c.   1st–5th c.   4th–8th c.   5th–7th c.   9th–12th c.   12th–15th c.   15th–16th c.   15th–16th c. (modern version)

© 2016 Getty-Dubay

LOWERCASE FAMILY 7 (o e c s)

OBJECTIVES: 45° pen angle, 5° slope. Review Family 1 to 6. Flatten pen angle slightly for s and z (ca. 30°).
Family 7 – Elliptical. Counter – elliptical shape – o. **Elliptical curve** left side – o e c.
Serifs: **soft angle exit serif** – c.
One-stroke – c s, **two**-stroke – o e.
Trace with pen just above solid black letters (almost touching); touch pen to paper for all other letters.

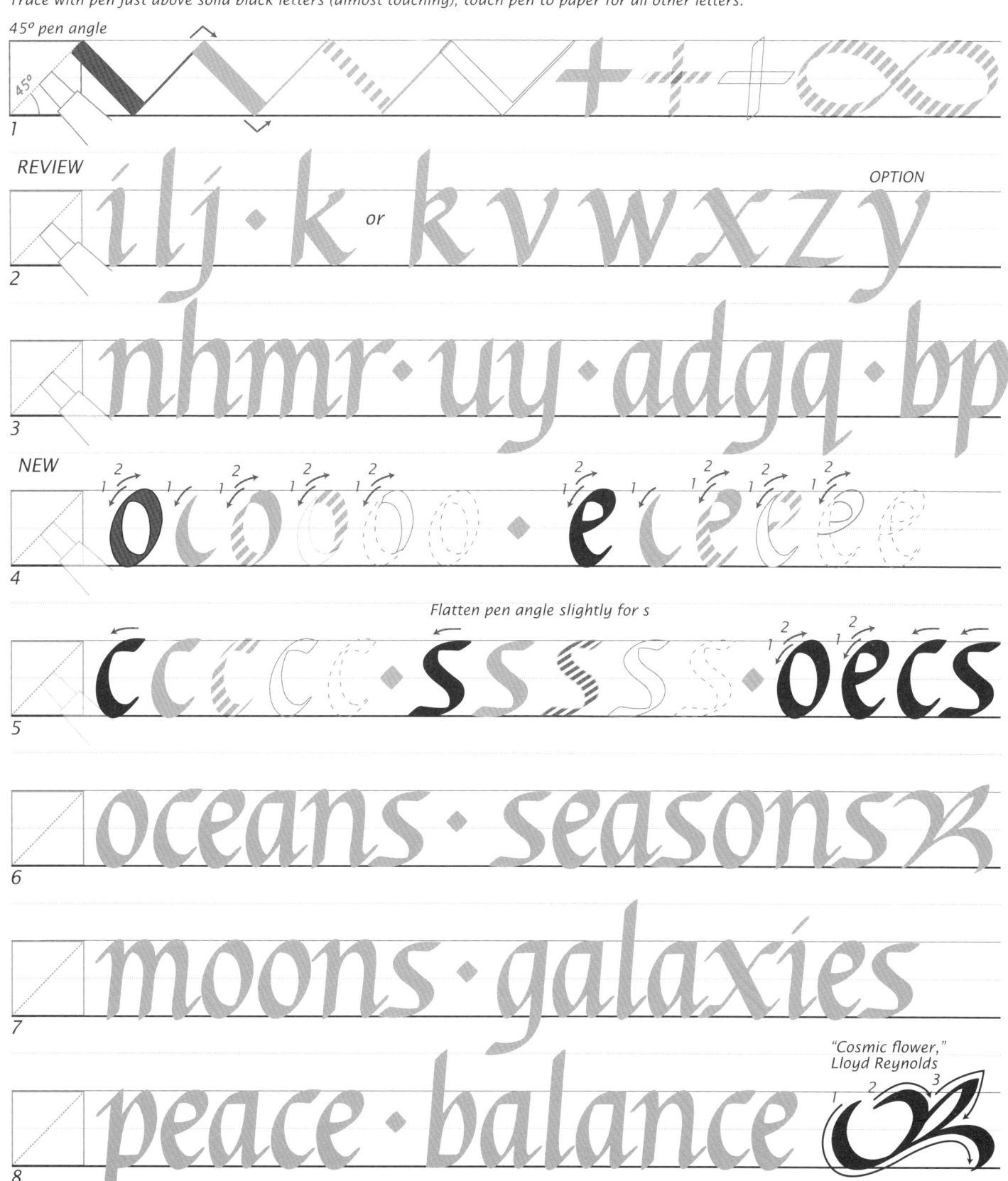

LOOK, PLAN, PRACTICE: **Look** for your personal best pen angle or best letter. Give yourself a star! Now, find a letter that you could improve. **Plan** how to improve—is it the pen angle or the letter shape? **Practice** the improved letter by writing it in a free space on the page.

DEVELOPMENT OF LOWERCASE FAMILY 8 (f t)

	Brush-written Roman Monumental Capitals (These examples are pen-written from letters incised in stone on Trajan's Column, Rome, 112–113 CE.)	Pen-written Roman Era Capitals			Pen-written Lowercase (used with capitals)					Date
		Square Capitals 0°	Rustic Capitals 85° 45°	Uncial Capitals 15°	Roman Half-Uncial 15°	Carolingian 30°	Black Letter 30°	Humanist 30°	Italic 45°	
	F	F	F	F	F	F	f	f	f	
	T	T	T	T	T	T	t	t	t	

TIMELINE: 1st–2nd c. CE   1st–5th c.   1st–5th c.   4th–8th c.   5th–7th c.   9th–12th c.   12th–15th c.   15th–16th c.   15th–16th c. (modern version)

© 2016 Getty-Dubay

LOWERCASE FAMILY 8 (f t)

OBJECTIVES: *45° pen angle, 5° slope.* Review Family 1 to 7. Flatten pen angle slightly for s, z, and crossbar of f and t (ca. 30°). Family 8 – **Crossbar.** Top of crossbar touches waistline and begins one pen width left of downstroke and ends when in line with top of f or bottom of t. **Ascender** – f curve left, t short. Serifs: **soft angle exit serif** – t. **Two-stroke** – f t.
Trace with pen just above solid black letters (almost touching); touch pen to paper for all other letters.

LOOK, PLAN, PRACTICE: Look for your personal best pen angle or best letter. Give yourself a star! Now, find a letter that you could improve. **Plan** how to improve—is it the pen angle or the letter shape? **Practice** the improved letter by writing it in a free space on the page.

© 2016 Getty-Dubay

REVIEW LOWERCASE, PANGRAM

OBJECTIVES: 45° pen angle, 5° slope. Review Family 1 to 8. Flatten pen angle slightly for s, z, and crossbar of f and t.
Pangram: A sentence containing the entire alphabet. **Letter spacing** in a word: two curves are close (almost touching), curve and downstroke more space, two downstrokes most space. **Word spacing** in a sentence: width of a sans-serif n between words.
Trace with pen just above solid black letters (almost touching); touch pen to paper for all other letters.

LOOK, PLAN, PRACTICE: Look for your personal best pen angle or best letter. Give yourself a star! Now, find a letter that you could improve. Plan how to improve—is it the pen angle or the letter shape? Practice the improved letter by writing it on a free space on the page.

REVIEW & PANGRAM (continued), PUNCTUATION

OBJECTIVES: 45° pen angle, 5° slope. Flatten pen angle slightly for s, z and crossbar of f and t. Pangram continued. Punctuation: exclamation mark, question mark, quotation marks, apostrophe, parentheses, period, dash, hyphen, semi-colon, and colon. Trace with pen just above solid black letters (almost touching); touch pen to paper for all other letters.

LOOK, PLAN, PRACTICE: Look for your personal best pen angle or best letter. Give yourself a star! Now, find a letter that you could improve. **Plan** how to improve—is it the pen angle or the letter shape? **Practice** the improved letter by writing it in a free space on the page.

© 2016 Getty-Dubay

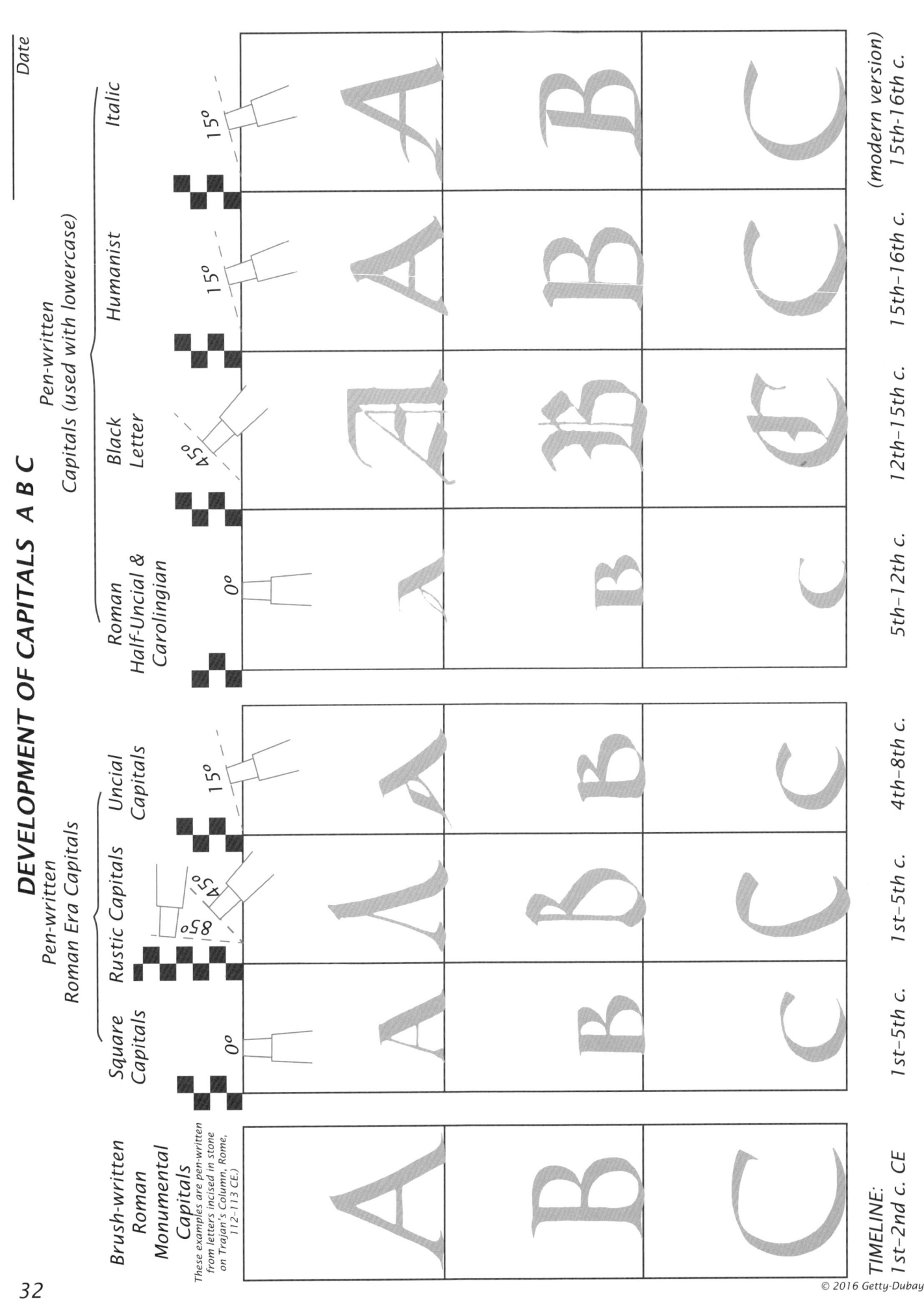

FORMAL CAPITALS A B C

OBJECTIVES: 15° pen angle. All capitals start at the top. Trace monoline capitals with pencil or finger.
A: 1st stroke – baseline serif; 2nd stroke – sharp exit serif; 3rd stroke – flourish horizontal.
B: 1st stroke – baseline serif horizontal; 2nd stroke – horizontal serif.
C: 1st stroke – full curve left; 2nd stroke – curve right.

EGYPTIAN	PHOENICIAN	GREEK EARLY / CLASSICAL	ROMAN
"ox"	aleph	alpha	A
"house"	beth	beta	B
"camel"	gimmel	gamma	C

Early Greek was bi-directional, written both right-to-left and left-to-right.

A quick brown dog jumps over the lazy fox.

LOOK, PLAN, PRACTICE: **Look** for your personal best pen angle or best letter. Give yourself a star! Now, find a letter that you could improve.
Plan how to improve—is it the pen angle or the letter shape? **Practice** the improved letter by writing it in a free space on the page.

© 2016 Getty-Dubay

FORMAL CAPITALS D E F

OBJECTIVES: 15° pen angle. All capitals start at the top. Trace monoline capitals with pencil or finger.
D: 1st stroke – baseline serif horizontal; 2nd stroke – horizontal serif.
E: 1st stroke – baseline serif horizontal; 2nd stroke – horizontal serif. 3rd stroke – horizontal.
F: 1st stroke – baseline exit serif; 2nd stroke – horizontal serif; 3rd stroke – horizontal.

EGYPTIAN   PHOENICIAN   GREEK EARLY CLASSICAL   ROMAN

daleth "door" — delta

he "look" or "behold" — epsilon

vau "hook" — digamma

Dd · Ee · Ff · Five jumping wizards hop quickly over the box. &

& = ampersand – Latin word "et": and

LOOK, PLAN, PRACTICE: Look for your personal best pen angle or best letter. Give yourself a star! Now, find a letter that you could improve. **Plan** how to improve—is it the pen angle or the letter shape? **Practice** the improved letter by writing it in a free space on the page.

© 2016 Getty-Dubay

FORMAL CAPITALS G H I

OBJECTIVES: 15° pen angle. All capitals start at the top. Trace monoline capitals with pencil or finger.
G: 1st stroke – full curve left; 2nd stroke – curve right; 3rd stroke – descender curve left.
H: 1st stroke – horizontal serif, baseline exit serif; 2nd stroke – serif curve left beginning higher than 1st stroke, sharp angle exit serif; 3rd stroke – flourish horizontal.
I: 1 stroke – entrance serif, baseline exit serif.

EGYPTIAN	PHOENICIAN	GREEK EARLY	GREEK CLASSICAL	ROMAN
	٦	＞＜	Γ	G
	gimmel "camel"		gamma	
	H	H	H	H
	heth "fence"		eta	
	ʓ	⟩⟨	ı	I
	yod "hand"		iota	

LOOK, PLAN, PRACTICE: Look for your personal best pen angle or best letter. Give yourself a star! Now, find a letter that you could improve. **Plan** how to improve—is it the pen angle or the letter shape? **Practice** the improved letter by writing it in a free space on the page.

© 2016 Getty-Dubay

DEVELOPMENT OF CAPITALS J K L

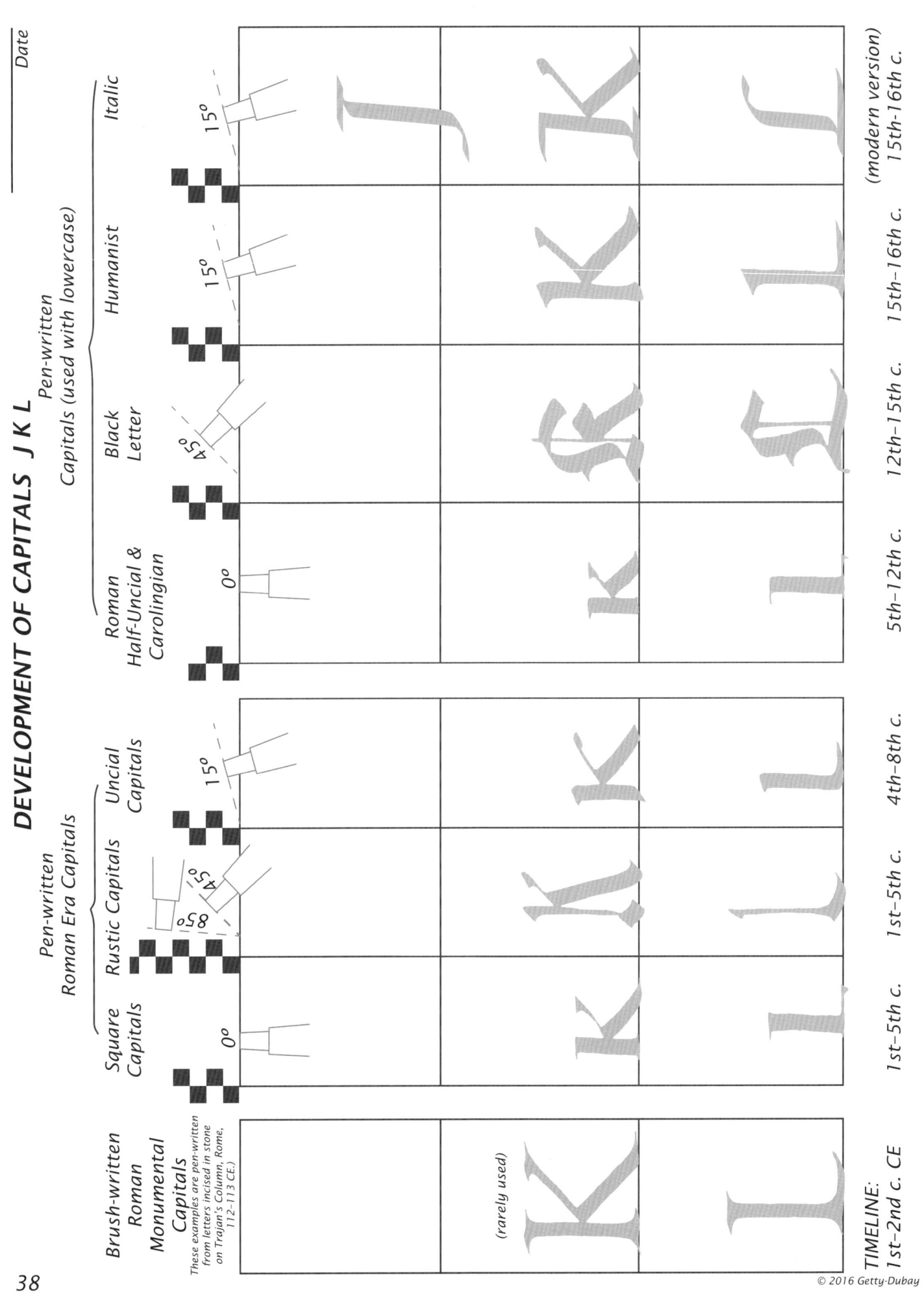

FORMAL CAPITALS J K L

OBJECTIVES: 15° pen angle. All capitals start at the top. Trace the monoline capitals with pencil or finger.
J: 1 stroke – entrance serif, descender curve left.
K: 1st stroke – horizontal serif, baseline exit serif; 2nd stroke – sharp angle entrance serif, soft angle exit serif.
L: 1 stroke – horizontal serif curve left, baseline serif horizontal.

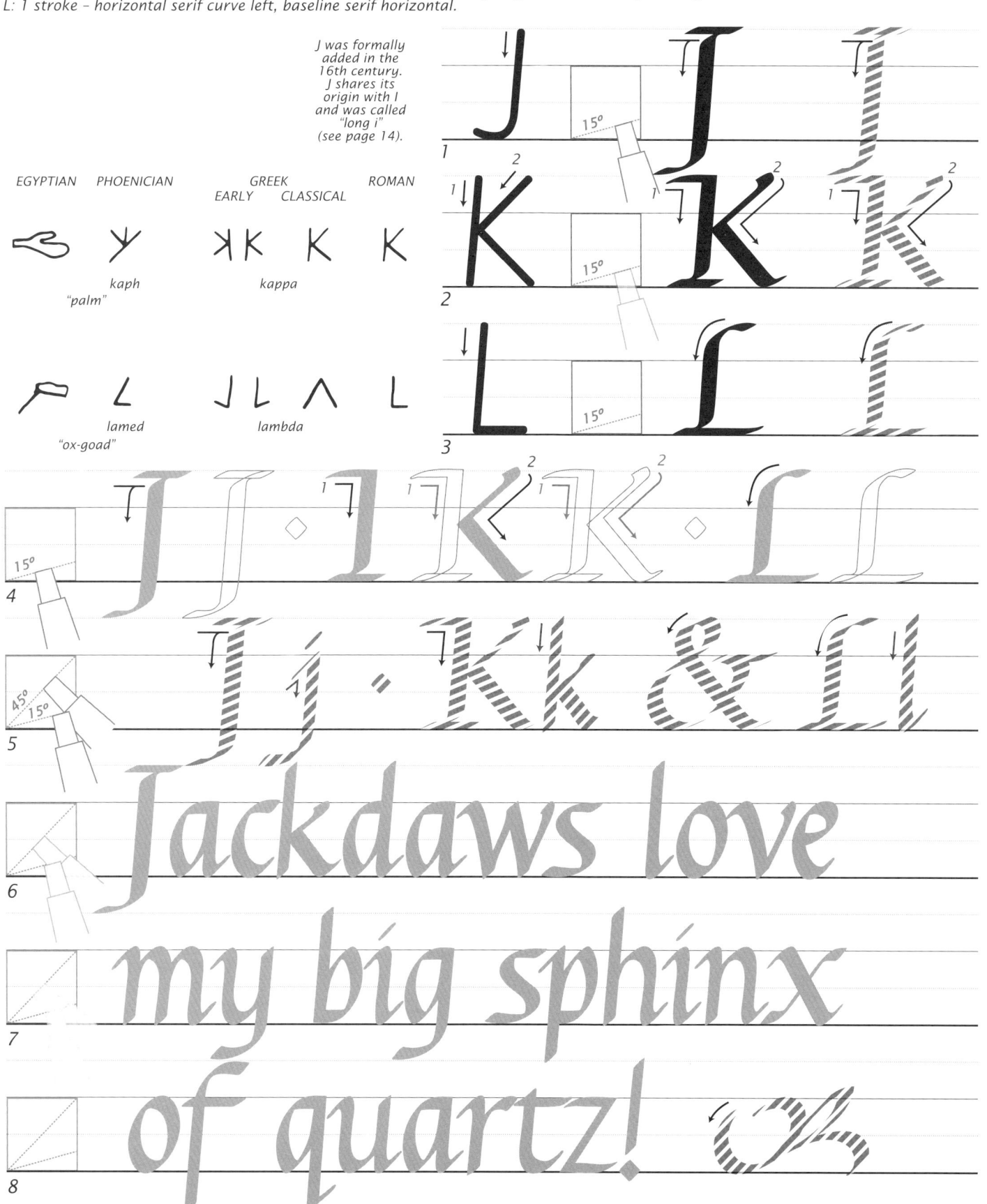

LOOK, PLAN, PRACTICE: **Look** for your personal best pen angle or best letter. Give yourself a star! Now, find a letter that you could improve.
Plan how to improve—is it the pen angle or the letter shape? **Practice** the improved letter by writing it in a free space on the page.

© 2016 Getty-Dubay

FORMAL CAPITALS M N O

OBJECTIVES: 15° pen angle. (See M and N for exceptions.) All capitals start at the top. Trace the monoline capitals with pencil or finger.
M: 1st stroke – horizontal serif 15° p.a., diagonal 45° p.a., baseline serif 15° p.a.; 2nd stroke – baseline exit serif 15° p.a.
N: 1st stroke – horizontal serif 15° p.a., downstroke 45° p.a., baseline exit serif 15° p.a.; 2nd stroke – diagonal 45° p.a.;
   3rd stroke – horizontal serif begins slightly higher than capital height curve left 15° p.a., downstroke 45° p.a.
O: 1st stroke – full curve left; 2nd stroke – full curve right.

EGYPTIAN	PHOENICIAN	GREEK EARLY	GREEK CLASSICAL	ROMAN
"water"	mem	mu		M
"fish"	nun	nu		N
"eye"	ayin	omicron		O

Letter M first diagonal downstroke use 45° pen angle.

Letter N downstrokes and diagonal use 45° pen angle.

15° pen angle for serifs

Many jackdaws quickly zip over the fox pen.

REVIEW: Steepen pen angle to 45° for first diagonal of M...
...other diagonals and serifs use 15° pen angle.

LOOK, PLAN, PRACTICE: Look for your personal best pen angle or best letter. Give yourself a star! Now, find a letter that you could improve.
Plan how to improve—is it the pen angle or the letter shape? **Practice** the improved letter by writing it in a free space on the page.

© 2016 Getty-Dubay

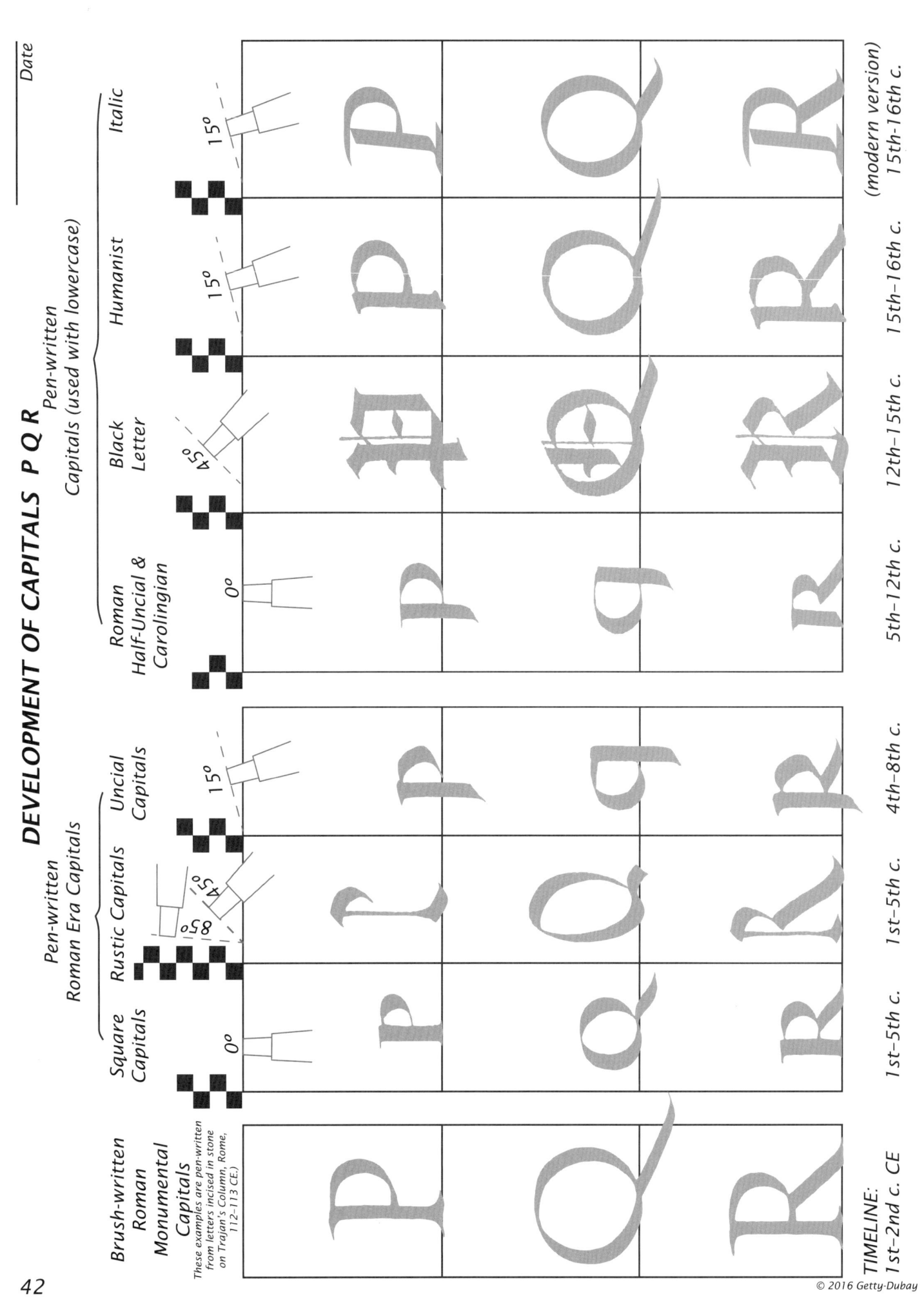

FORMAL CAPITALS P Q R

OBJECTIVES: 15° pen angle. All capitals start at the top. Trace the monoline capitals with pencil or finger.
R: 1st stroke – baseline exit serif; 2nd – horizontal entrance serif, curve right; 3rd – horizontal; 4th stroke – soft angle exit serif.
Q: 1st stroke – full curve left; 2nd stroke – full curve right; 3rd stroke – soft angle serif.
P: 1st stroke – baseline exit serif; 2nd stroke – horizontal serif.

EGYPTIAN	PHOENICIAN	GREEK EARLY	GREEK CLASSICAL	ROMAN
"mouth"	pe	ꥤ	π pi	P
	qoph "knot"	φ	koppa	Q
"head"	resh		rho	R

"Quick wafting zephyrs vex bold Jim," they said.

LOOK, PLAN, PRACTICE: Look for your personal best pen angle or best letter. Give yourself a star! Now, find a letter that you could improve.
Plan how to improve—is it the pen angle or the letter shape? **Practice** the improved letter by writing it in a free space on the page.

FORMAL CAPITALS S T U

OBJECTIVES: **15° pen angle.** All capitals start at the top. Trace the monoline capitals with pencil or finger.
S: 1st stroke – curve left, diagonal, curve right, curve left; 2nd stroke – curve right.
T: 1st stroke – baseline exit serif; 2nd stroke – slight horizontal entrance and exit serifs.
U: 1st stroke – horizontal serif; 2nd stroke – sharp angle exit serif.
4th stroke – soft angle exit serif.

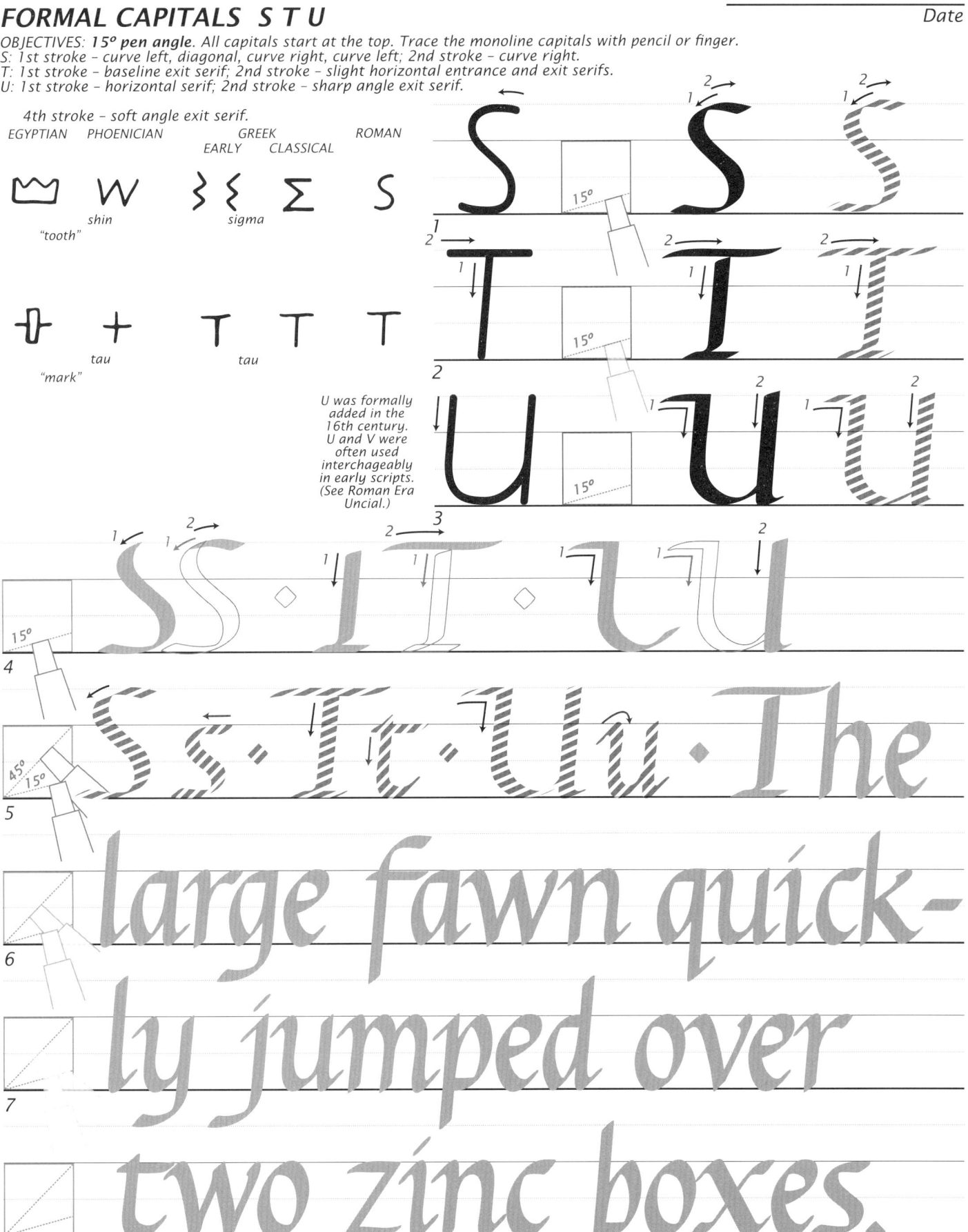

U was formally added in the 16th century. U and V were often used interchageably in early scripts. (See Roman Era Uncial.)

LOOK, PLAN, PRACTICE: Look for your personal best pen angle or best letter. Give yourself a star! Now, find a letter that you could improve. **Plan** how to improve—is it the pen angle or the letter shape? **Practice** the improved letter by writing it in a free space on the page.

© 2016 Getty-Dubay

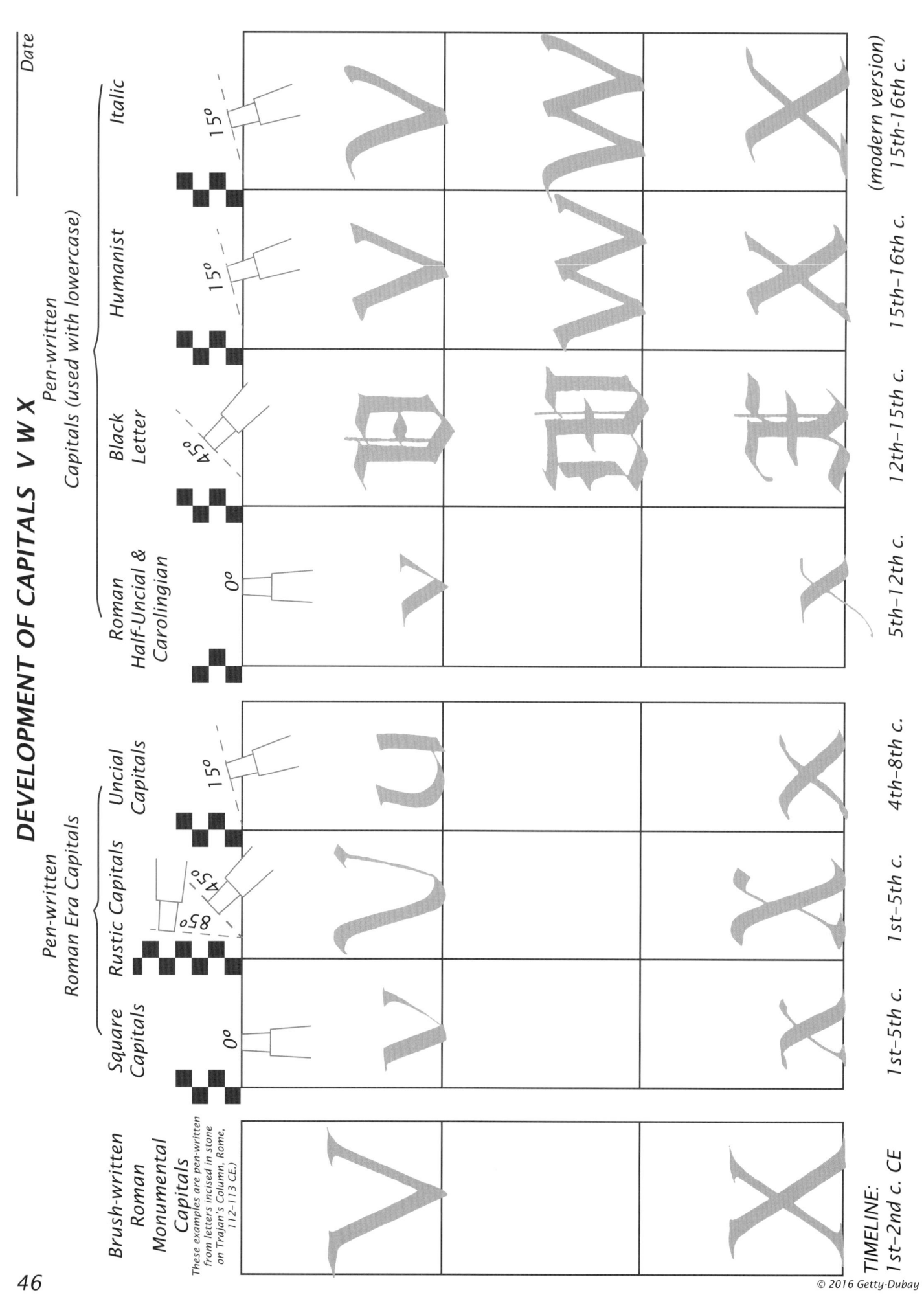

FORMAL CAPITALS V W X

OBJECTIVES: 15° pen angle. *All capitals start at the top. Trace the monoline capitals with pencil or finger.*
V: 1 stroke – soft angle entrance serif, sharp angle exit serif.
W: 1 stroke – soft angle entrance serif, sharp angle exit serif.
X: 1st stroke – soft angle entrance serif, soft angle exit serif; 2nd stroke – horizontal entrance serif, horizontal exit serif.

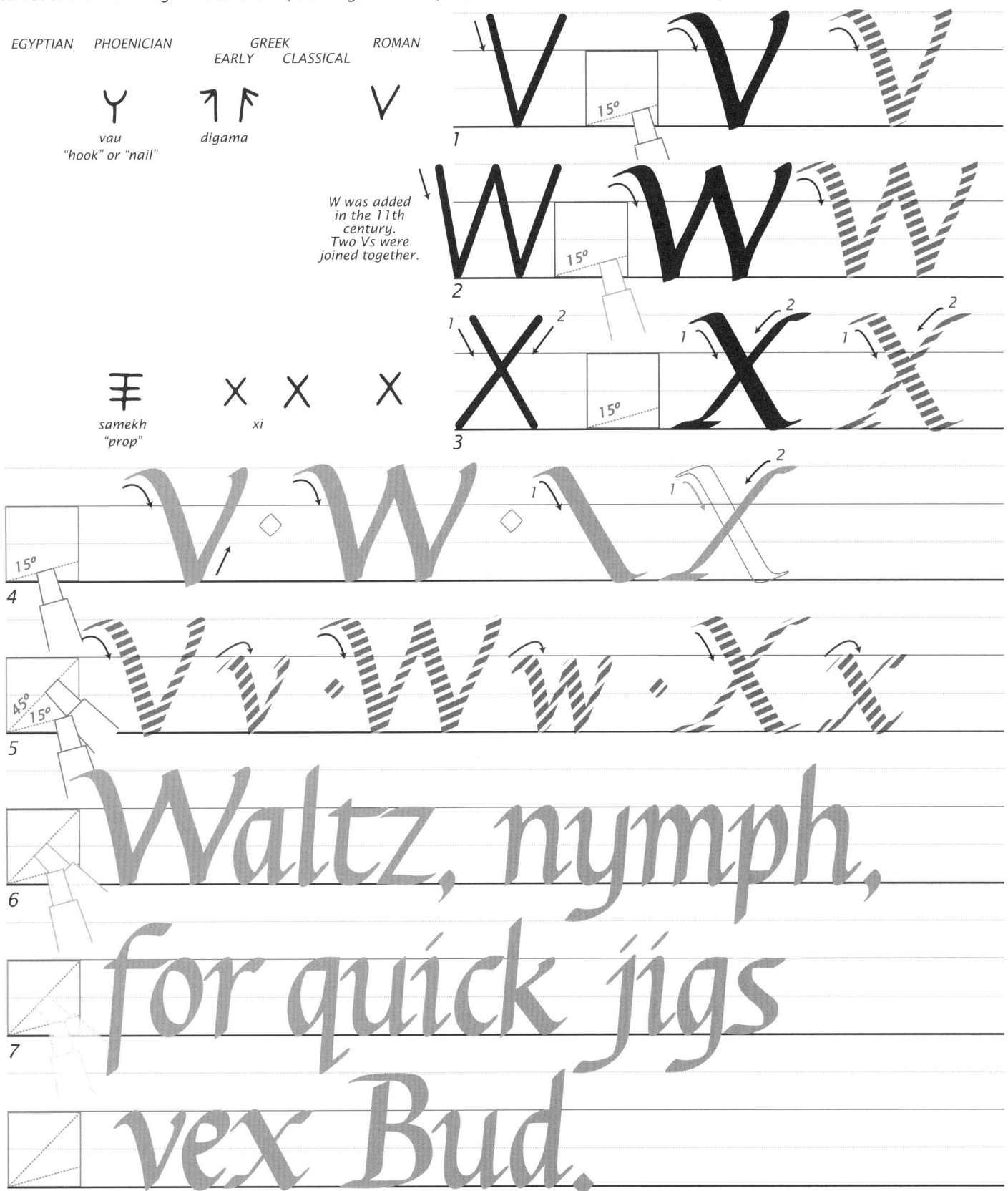

LOOK, PLAN, PRACTICE: **Look** *for your personal best pen angle or best letter. Give yourself a star! Now, find a letter that you could improve.*
Plan *how to improve—is it the pen angle or the letter shape?* **Practice** *the improved letter by writing it in a free space on the page.*

© 2016 Getty-Dubay

47

DEVELOPMENT OF CAPITALS Y Z

Date _____

Brush-written Roman Monumental Capitals
These examples are pen-written from letters incised in stone on Trajan's Column, Rome, 112–113 CE.

Pen-written Roman Era Capitals
- Square Capitals (0°)
- Rustic Capitals (85°/45°)
- Uncial Capitals (15°)

Pen-written Capitals (used with lowercase)
- Roman Half-Uncial & Carolingian (0°)
- Black Letter (45°)
- Humanist (15°)
- Italic (15°)

Greek letter upsilon added 1st c. BCE

Greek letter zeta added 1st c. BCE

TIMELINE: 1st–2nd c. CE | 1st–5th c. | 1st–5th c. | 4th–8th c. | 5th–12th c. | 12th–15th c. | 15th–16th c. | (modern version) 15th–16th c.

48

© 2016 Getty-Dubay

FORMAL CAPITALS Y Z

OBJECTIVES: 15° pen angle. All capitals start at the top. Trace the monoline capitals with pencil or finger.
Y: 1st stroke – horizontal serif; 2nd stroke – descender curve left.
OPTION Y: 1st stroke – soft angle entrance serif; 2nd stroke – sharp angle entrance serif, descender curve left.
Z: 1 stroke – slight horizontal entrance serif and exit serif.

EGYPTIAN	PHOENICIAN	GREEK EARLY	GREEK CLASSICAL	ROMAN
	Y	Y	Y	Y
	vau "hook" or "nail"		upsilon	
ᒣ	Z	I	Z	Z
zayin "sickle" or "weapon"		zeta		

OPTION

Zak's frowzy
things plumb
vex'd Jack Q.

LOOK, PLAN, PRACTICE: **Look** for your personal best pen angle or best letter. Give yourself a star! Now, find a letter that you could improve.
Plan how to improve—is it the pen angle or the letter shape? **Practice** the improved letter by writing it in a free space on the page.

HINDU-ARABIC NUMERALS

Date

0 1 2 3 4 5 6 7 8 9

- 0: meaning "empty"
- 4: N/W/E/S compass
- 6, 8, and 9: origins are unknown
- 7: shape possibly from stars in the Big Dipper constellation

Hindu-Arabic numerals originated in India in the 1st to 4th centuries. Hindu mathematicians invented the zero, meaning "empty." (Roman numerals had no zero.) Arab mathematicians learned the Hindu system and later assisted its spread to Europe. It did not have widespread use until the 1500s.

Leonardo Fibonacci, ca. 1175–1240, was born in Pisa, Italy. His father, a merchant, took him to northern Africa where he learned Hindu-Arabic numerals. Leonardo introduced this system to Europe. His book, Liber Abaci, written in 1202, showed how to do arithmetic in the decimal system, techniques of algebra, and the theory of quadratic equations.

OBJECTIVES: 15° pen angle for numerals. All numerals start at the top.

1. 0 0 0 1 1 2 2 2 3 3 4 4 4

2. 5 5 5 6 6 6 7 7 or 7 7 7

3. 8 8 or 8 8 8 9 9 9 ∞ *infinity*

4. 0 1 2 3 4 5 6 7 or 7 8 9

5. 0 1 2 3 4 5 6 7 or 7 8 9

6. 0 1 2 3 4 5 6 7 or 7 8 9

NOTE: For these mathematical symbols, use a 15° pen angle.

7. + − × ÷ < ( ) = π

45° pen angle for @

Latin word "ad": at
ad or a∂ becomes @

@

LOOK, PLAN, PRACTICE: **Look** for your personal best pen angle or best numeral. Give yourself a star! Now, find a numeral that you could improve. **Plan** how to improve—is it the pen angle or the shape? **Practice** the improved letter by writing it in a free space on the page.

REVIEW & LIGATURES

OBJECTIVES: Introduction to 2mm nib; 15° pen angle (except N) – capitals; 45° pen angle – lowercase (except s, crossbar of f and t); Ligatures – connect out of crossbar of f and t (flatten pen angle slightly for crossbar).
NOTE: Only use formal capitals in combination with lowercase letters. For words in all capitals, use plain capitals (see page 52).

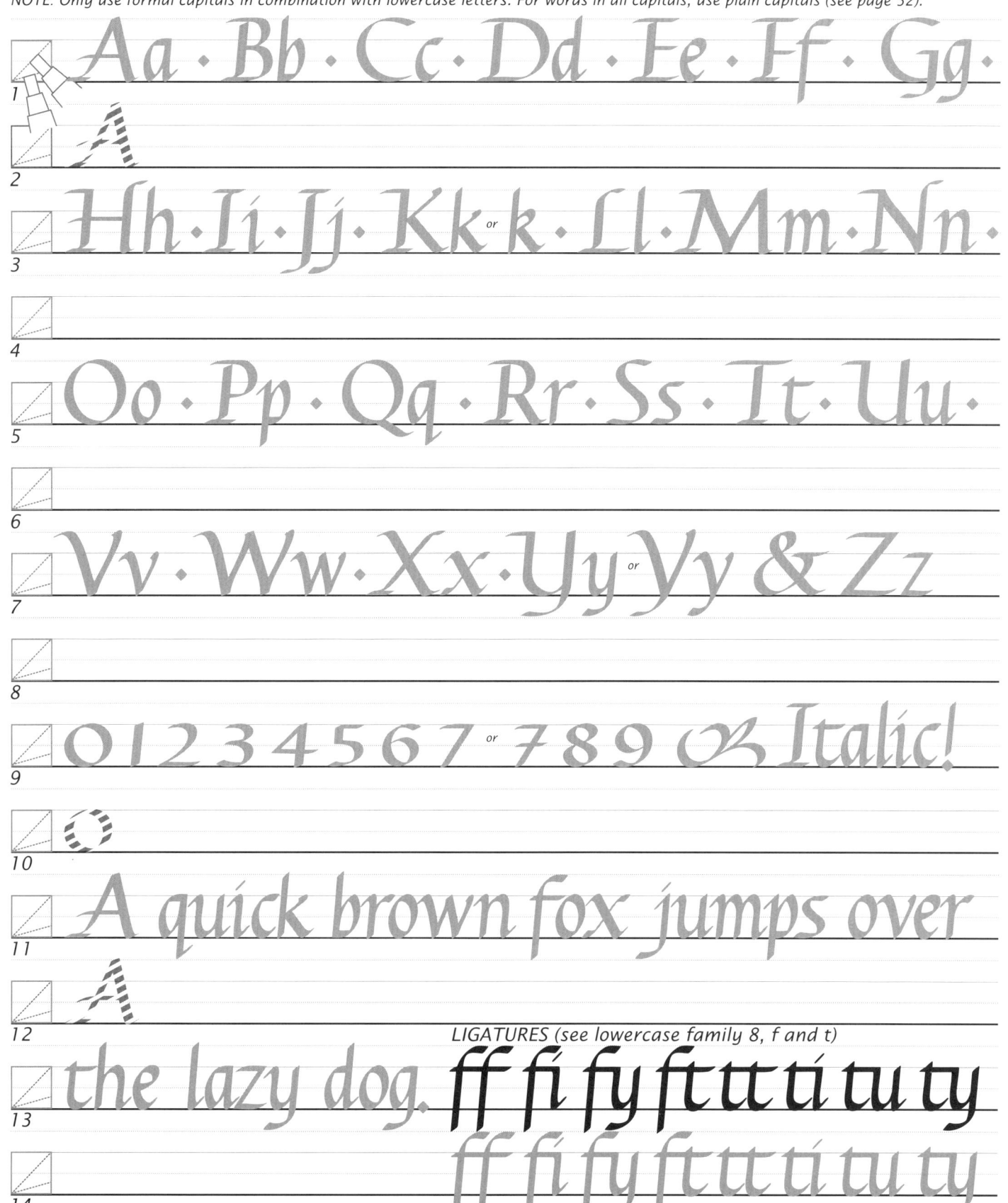

Aa · Bb · Cc · Dd · Ee · Ff · Gg ·

Hh · Ii · Jj · Kk or k · Ll · Mm · Nn ·

Oo · Pp · Qq · Rr · Ss · Tt · Uu ·

Vv · Ww · Xx · Yy or Yy & Zz

0 1 2 3 4 5 6 7 or 7 8 9 & Italic!

A quick brown fox jumps over the lazy dog.

LIGATURES (see lowercase family 8, f and t)

ff fi fy ft tt ti tu ty

ff fi fy ft tt ti tu ty

LOOK, PLAN, PRACTICE: Look for your personal best pen angle or best letter. Give yourself a star! Now, find a letter that you could improve. **Plan** how to improve—is it the pen angle or the letter shape? **Practice** the improved letter by writing it in a free space on the page.

© 2016 Getty-Dubay

PLAIN CAPITALS, SMALL CAPITALS & MIXED CAPITALS

Date

OBJECTIVES: Plain Capitals – 15° pen angle. Used in titles, credits and acronyms. Stroke sequence is the same as with Formal Capitals (first stroke is indicated). Use mixed capitals (plain capitals combined with small capitals) for titles.
Trace with pen just above solid black letters (almost touching); touch pen to paper for all other letters.

45° pen angle for first stroke of M

1 A B C D E F G H I J L K M
2 A B C D E F G H I J L K M

45° pen angle for N

3 N O P Q R S T U V W X Y Z
4 N O P Q R S T U V W X Y Z
5 A B C D E F G H I J K L M N O P Q
6 A B C D E F G H I J K L M N O P Q
7 R S T U V W X Y Z MIXED CAPS
8 R S T U V W X Y Z M
9 THE GOLDEN RULE
10 T
11 Do to others as you would
12 have others do to you.
13 Do
14

LOOK, PLAN, PRACTICE: **Look** for your personal best pen angle or best letter. Give yourself a star! Now, find a letter that you could improve. **Plan** how to improve—is it the pen angle or the letter shape? **Practice** the improved letter by writing it in a free space on the page.

POEM

OBJECTIVES: **15° pen angle** – capitals; **45° pen angle** – lowercase (except s, crossbar of f and t); ligatures fi and ty.
Use mixed capitals (plain capitals combined with small capitals) for credits.

Date

1–2. To see a world in a grain of sand
3. T
4. i
5. And a heaven in a wild flower,
6. A
7–8. Hold infinity in the palm of your hand
9. H
10. O
11. And eternity in an hour.
12. A
13. WILLIAM BLAKE
14. W

England, 1767–1827 · "Auguries of Innocence"

LOOK, PLAN, PRACTICE: **Look** for your personal best pen angle or best letter. Give yourself a star! Now, find a letter that you could improve. **Plan** how to improve—is it the pen angle or the letter shape? **Practice** the improved letter by writing it in a free space on the page.

QUOTATIONS

OBJECTIVES: **15° pen angle** – *capitals;* **45° pen angle** – *lowercase (except s, crossbar of f and t); ligature tr.*
Use mixed capitals (plain capitals combined with small capitals) for titles and credits.

Date

1. All's Well That Ends Well
2. A
3. Love all, trust few, do wrong
4. to none. L
5.
6. Romeo & Juliet
7. R
8. That which we call a rose by
9. any other name would smell as
10. sweet. T
11.
12.
13. William Shakespeare
14. W

England, 1564-1616

LOOK, PLAN, PRACTICE: Look for your personal best pen angle or best letter. Give yourself a star! Now, find a letter that you could improve.
Plan how to improve—is it the pen angle or the letter shape? **Practice** the improved letter by writing it in a free space on the page.

QUOTATIONS
Date

OBJECTIVES: **15° pen angle** – capitals; **45° pen angle** – lowercase (except s, crossbar of f and t); ligatures tr and fr.
Use mixed capitals (plain capitals combined with small capitals) for credits.

Kind words can be short and easy to speak, but their echoes are truly endless. Ki

MOTHER TERESA
M

1910-1997 · Nobel Peace Prize 1979

Love is the only force capable of transforming an enemy into a friend. L

MARTIN LUTHER KING, JR.
M

1929-1968 · Nobel Peace Prize 1964

LOOK, PLAN, PRACTICE: Look for your personal best pen angle or best letter. Give yourself a star! Now, find a letter that you could improve. **Plan** how to improve—is it the pen angle or the letter shape? **Practice** the improved letter by writing it in a free space on the page.

© 2016 Getty-Dubay

55

GREEK & LATIN ROOT WORDS

OBJECTIVES: **15° pen angle** – capitals; **45° pen angle** – lowercase (except s, crossbar of f and t); ligatures ti and fu.

Date _____

root word — meaning in English — root word in English word

GREEK

1. kalos (beautiful) – calligraphy
2.
3. grapho (draw, write) – graphic
4.
5. photos (light) – photography
6.

LATIN

7. currere (to run) – cursive
8.
9. scribere (to write) – inscribe
10.
11. manus (hand) – manuscript
12.
13. verbum (word) – verbal
14.

LOOK, PLAN, PRACTICE: **Look** for your personal best pen angle or best letter. Give yourself a star! Now, find a letter that you could improve. **Plan** how to improve—is it the pen angle or the letter shape? **Practice** the improved letter by writing it in a free space on the page.

50 MOST USED ENGLISH WORDS

OBJECTIVES: *15° pen angle* – capitals; *45° pen angle* – lowercase (except s, crossbar of f and t); ligature fr.
NOTE: These most frequently used English words are listed in order of usage.

Date

the · be · to · of · and · a · in · that ·

have · I · it · for · not · on · with · he ·

as · you · do · at · this · but · his · by ·

from · they · we · say · her · she · or ·

an · will · my · one · all · would ·

there · their · what · so · up · out · if

about · who · get · which · go · me ·

(Source: Wikipedia)

LOOK, PLAN, PRACTICE: **Look** for your personal best pen angle or best letter. Give yourself a star! Now, find a letter that you could improve. **Plan** how to improve—is it the pen angle or the letter shape? **Practice** the improved letter by writing it in a free space on the page.

© 2016 Getty-Dubay

CARDS & LETTERS, FLOURISHED CAPITALS & LOWERCASE

OBJECTIVES: 15° pen angle – capitals; **45° pen angle** – lowercase (except s, z, and crossbar of f and t). OPTION: Flourished ascenders on b d h k l as on f with added height for all six ascenders; Flourished descenders on f and p as on g j y with added length for all six descenders including q. (With flourished ascenders & descenders use every other line on ruled lines, pages 61 and 64.) Optional flourish on e at end of sentence or end of person's name. Flourished capitals – H K M N U Y begin with flourish, B D E F P R T begin with downstroke.

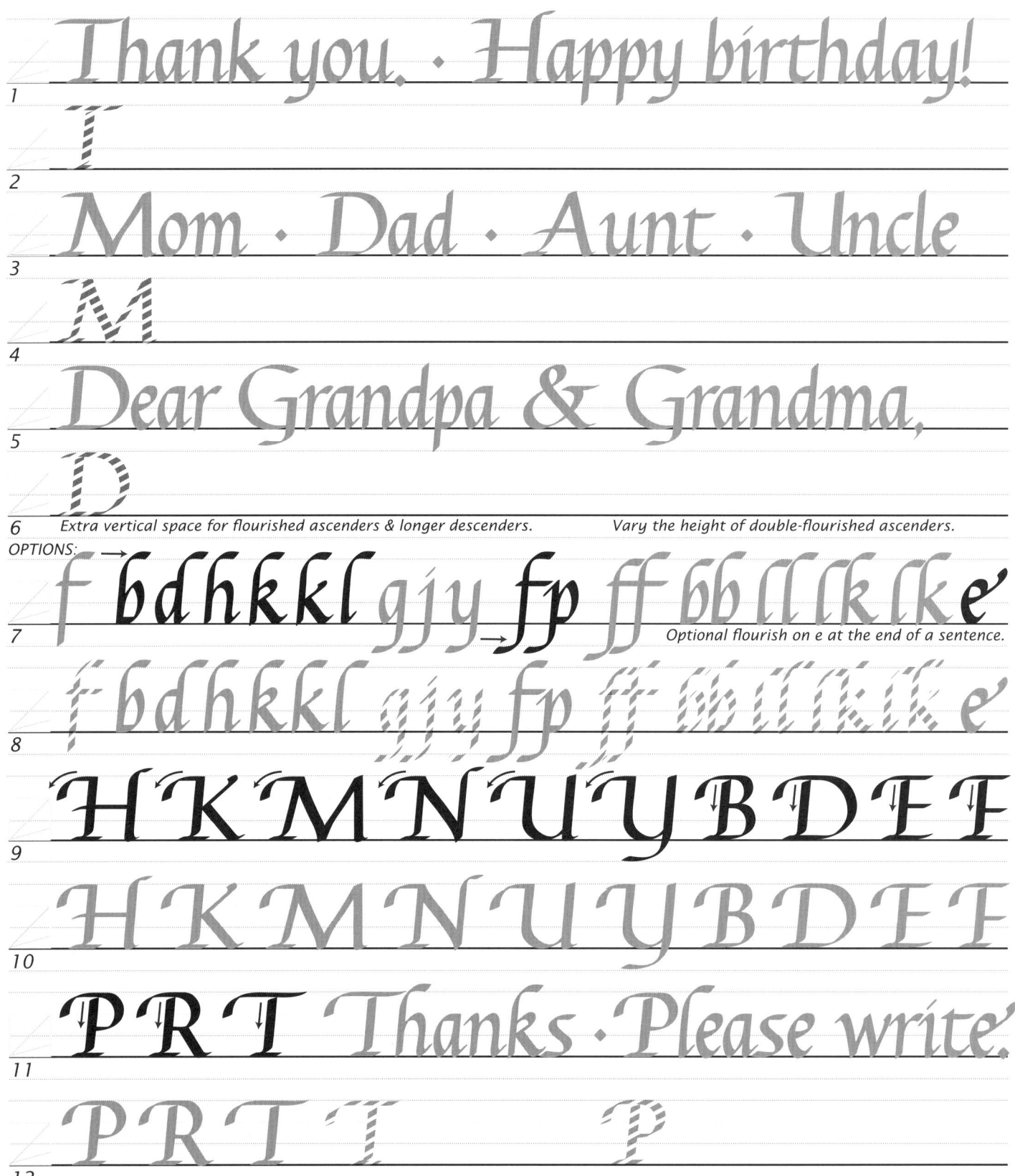

Extra vertical space for flourished ascenders & longer descenders.   Vary the height of double-flourished ascenders.

OPTIONS:

Optional flourish on e at the end of a sentence.

LOOK, PLAN, PRACTICE: Look for your personal best pen angle or best letter. Give yourself a star! Now, find a letter that you could improve. **Plan** how to improve — is it the pen angle or the letter shape? **Practice** the improved letter by writing it in a free space on the page.

CURSIVE ITALIC

OBJECTIVES: 15° pen angle – capitals; **45° pen angle** – lowercase (except s, z, crossbar of f and t). Presenting 8 possible cursive joins & options, including lifts. JOIN 1: Diagonal; JOIN 2: Swing up; JOIN 3: Diagonal, start back (diagonal out of 2nd stroke of e); JOIN 4: Diagonal into optional one-stroke e; or lift. JOIN 5: Horizontal (Note: slightly flattened pen angle); JOIN 6: Diagonal into r, or lift; JOIN 7: Horizontal into diagonal, or lift; JOIN 8: Diagonal into horizontal, or lift.

1. JOIN 1 — an am ar ax · OPTION: use JOIN 2 — an am ar ax · JOIN 2 — au
2. an
3. ay ai at aj ap av aw al ah ab ak or ak
4. a
5. JOIN 3 — ao aen · JOIN 4 OPTION — ae ae · JOIN 5 — on tn fn vn wn xn
6. ao
7. JOIN 4 OPTION — rn rn · JOIN 7 — sn bn pn OPTION — sn bn pn · JOIN 8 (or lift) — aa ac
8. rn
9. ad ag aq as · LIFTS — af az · gu ju qu yu
10. ad
11. A quick brown fox jumps over
12. A
13. the lazy dog. Cursive italic is
14. i

LOOK, PLAN, PRACTICE.
Congratulations! After completing this book, print out a Certificate of Completion by visiting www.handwritingsuccess.com.

DEVELOPMENT OF LOWERCASE

_____ Date

Pen-written Lowercase (used with capitals)

Roman Half-Uncial — 15°
Carolingian — 30°
Black Letter — 30°
Humanist — 30°
Italic — 45°

Pen-written Roman Era Capitals

Square Capitals — 0°
Rustic Capitals — 85° / 45°
Uncial Capitals — 15°

Brush-written Roman Monumental Capitals

TIMELINE: 1st–2nd c. CE | 1st–5th c. | 1st–5th c. | 4th–8th c. | 5th–7th c. | 9th–12th c. | 12th–15th c. | 15th–16th c. | 15th–16th c. (modern version)

45° pen angle

1

2

3

4

5

6

7

8

LOOK, PLAN, PRACTICE: Look for your personal best pen angle or best letter. Give yourself a star! Now, find a letter that you could improve. **Plan** how to improve—is it the pen angle or the letter shape? **Practice** the improved letter by writing it in a free space on the page.

DEVELOPMENT OF CAPITALS

Date _____

Brush-written Roman Monumental Capitals			
Pen-written Roman Era Capitals — Square Capitals (0°)			
Rustic Capitals (85°/45°)			
Uncial Capitals (15°)			
Pen-written Capitals (used with lowercase) — Roman Half-Uncial & Carolingian (0°)			
Black Letter (45°)			
Humanist (15°)			
Italic (15°)			

TIMELINE:
1st–2nd c. CE | 1st–5th c. | 1st–5th c. | 4th–8th c. | 5th–12th c. | 12th–15th c. | 15th–16th c. | 15th–16th c. (modern version)

Date

EGYPTIAN   PHOENICIAN   GREEK   ROMAN
                      EARLY   CLASSICAL

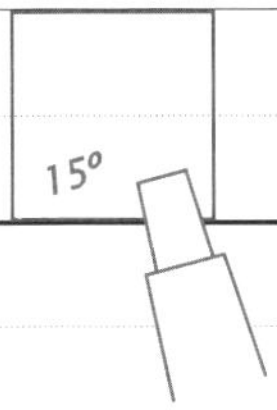

1

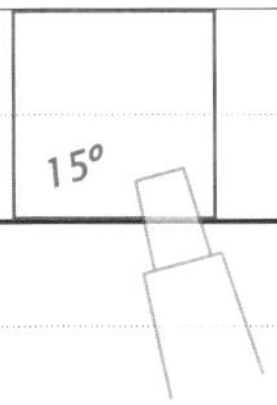

2

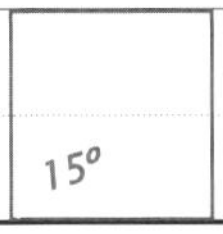

3

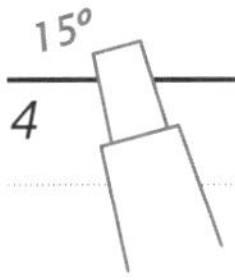

4

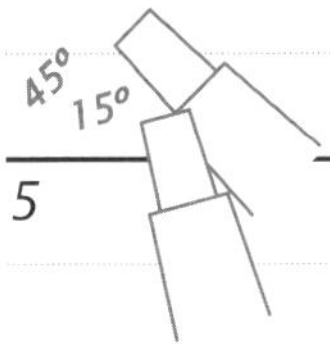

5

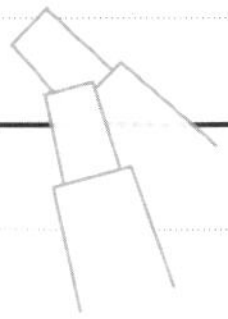

6

7

8

LOOK, PLAN, PRACTICE: **Look** for your personal best pen angle or best letter. Give yourself a star! Now, find a letter that you could improve. **Plan** how to improve—is it the pen angle or the letter shape? **Practice** the improved letter by writing it in a free space on the page.

Date

LOOK, PLAN, PRACTICE: **Look** for your personal best pen angle or best letter. Give yourself a star! Now, find a letter that you could improve. **Plan** how to improve—is it the pen angle or the letter shape? **Practice** the improved letter by writing it in a free space on the page.

64   Getty-Dubay Productions, www.handwritingsuccess.com